The Exodus Keys

Unlocking the Mysteries of the Great Tribulation

by
David Mathews

Foreword by
John-James of the House of Flores.®

CCB Publishing
British Columbia, Canada

The Exodus Keys: Unlocking the Mysteries of the Great Tribulations

Copyright ©2021 by David Mathews
ISBN-13   978-1-77143-496-6
First Edition

Library and Archives Canada Cataloguing in Publication
Title: The exodus keys : unlocking the mysteries of the great tribulations / by David Mathews.
Names: Mathews, David, 1958- author.
Description: First edition.
ISBN 9781771434966 (softcover) | ISBN 9781771434973 (PDF)
Additional cataloguing data is available from Library and Archives Canada.

All Scriptural quotes are from the 1987 version of the KJV Bible and are in the Public Domain.

All other authors' quotes or materials written or otherwise contained herein are quoted by permission and/or are in the Public Domain.

All images contained herein are reproduced by permission from the copyright holder or are in the Public Domain.

Cover artwork credit: © Simon Wong
Email: simon-wong@live.co.uk / Website: www.simon-wong.co.uk

The Hebrew fonts contained within are from BibleWorks.
"BWHEBB, BWHEBL, BWTRANSH [Hebrew]; BWGRKL, BWGRKN, and BWGRKI [Greek] PostScript® Type 1 and TrueType fonts Copyright ©1994-2013 BibleWorks, LLC. All rights reserved. These Biblical Greek and Hebrew fonts are used with permission and are from BibleWorks (www.bibleworks.com).

Extreme care has been taken by the author to ensure that all information presented in this book is accurate and up to date at the time of publishing. Neither the author nor the publisher can be held responsible for any errors or omissions. Additionally, neither is any liability assumed for damages resulting from the use of the information contained herein.

All rights reserved. No part of this publication may be reproduced, stored in a retrieval system or transmitted in any form or by any means, electronic, mechanical, photocopying, recording or otherwise without the express written permission of the author, except in the case of excerpts used in brief reviews or publications.

For information regarding written permission or for author interviews please contact:
Manna from Heaven Ministries
7488 Mt. Angel Hwy NE
Silverton, OR   97381
www.livingmanna.net

Publisher: CCB Publishing
                 British Columbia, Canada
                 www.ccbpublishing.com

Acknowledgements

This has been an exciting journey! We've discovered some wonderful hidden Truths and I couldn't have accomplished the task without the concerted efforts of those who bore this burden with me! Again, I want to give credit to my lovely bride of 28 years, Brenda. She more than anyone has stiffened my backbone so that I was able to tolerate the criticism and character assassination from those who viewed my perspective regarding the plagues as incredulous! She encouraged me and prayed for me! Thank you Brenda.

My children who were daily here at the MannaCrew Bunker: B.J. and Joy and her new husband Michael gave me valuable feedback and endured the ride! Brandy, Daniel, Rebecca & Matt, Renisha and Candace, hugs to ya'll as well!

My greatest protégé Brittney for her tireless efforts in support of our Vision!

Finally, my Brother and Co-Pastor John-James of the House of Flores.® and his wife Rochelle for standing with us, taking much of the Pastoral load and challenging me to dig deeper. Thank you for your priceless gift to our family – your friendship.

The Cover artwork is credited to Simon Wong who has been so gracious to create these images and share his gifting with us! He is simply amazing!

E-mail: SIMON-WOMG@LIVE.CO.UK
Facebook: https://www.facebook.com/simonwongart

In addition, the artwork illustrating the 10 plagues within the body of the book is that of Sabine Alex:

http://www.torah-illustrations.blogspot.com

Another wonderful Sister who has so graced us with her brilliant concepts of the 10 plagues!

Disclaimer

This book is designed to provoke you, the Reader, to dig beyond the surface level of religious traditions. Especially as it relates to the subject of this work: The Coming Great Tribulation as seen through the lens of the Exodus plagues! We have covered many topics that will no doubt stir controversy to a new level as we knocked over the Sacred Cows of theological perspective, which long stood against a proper understanding of what is about to happen. There will be some who may argue against my Hebraic scholarship and assume I took textural license in order to make my perspective fit. That's fine, truth can stand scrutiny! I have more than 35 years in ministry, 24 of which found us in a Torah based, Hebrew mindset, without which much of what I've shared would still be hidden. We're by no means experts in many of the areas that I will call attention to, yet we've spent two decades studying the Language of Creation, written and published several books and magazine and newspaper articles and endured countless hours of television and radio scrutiny from our peers. Finally, though I am certain The Creator inspires the work within, and that much of it is newly seen prophetic revelation, I cannot take personal credit for the contents. I merely held the pen and took dictation as the Holy Spirit; the Ruach H'Qodesh led us to new heights and deeper depths. I caution you to continue reading at your own risk else you will be held accountable by Him for what you're going to find!

Unleash The Hounds!

David Mathews

Books by David Mathews

The Rainbow Language:
The Sight, Sound & Color of the Holy Tongue
Published 2015 – ISBN 9781771432399

The Serpent's Seed:
They're Among Us
Published 2016 – ISBN 9781771432856

Ezekiel's Wheel Within A Wheel
Published 2020 – ISBN 9781771434256

The Exodus Keys
Published 2021 – ISBN 9781771434966

Contents

Foreword xi
Preface xv

Chapter 1: The Plagues of the Great Tribulation:
The Exodus Connection 1

Chapter 2: The Plague of Frogs 12

Chapter 3: The 4th Plague: Swarms of Flies 33

Chapter 4: Where's the Proof? Hidden Agendas
Revealed 48

Chapter 5: The Nimrod-Cain-Esau Connection 67

Chapter 6: The 7th Plague: Grievous Hail 78

Chapter 7: Who Exactly Is Cut Off? 96

Chapter 8: The 8th Plague: Locusts 116

Chapter 9: The 9th Plague: Darkness 125

Chapter 10: Lailah and Heylel 132

Chapter 11: The 10th Plague: Death and the Firstborn 151

Chapter 12: The Red Sea Crossing – The Exodus
Plagues Continued 174

Foreword

- 1John 2:18 "Little children, it is the last hour of the season. And as you have heard already that the anti-messiah is coming, even now many anti-messiahs have manifested. This is how we know that it is the last hour."

We have been given many signs in the Scriptures regarding End time events and it just seems like these very signs have been unfolding more and more at a rapid and unusual pace all the world can agree to. Layer upon layer, things seem to be unfolding from the prophetic library of Heavens chambers here on the Earth. We have seen the events of Matthew 24 materialize over and over, from one level to the next. Yeshua said these things - these events will not overtake those of us as a thief, who has ears to hear what the Spirit is saying and revealing to the laborers in the field of truth and revelation?

Over the centuries many scholars and learned men on all eschatological platforms have tried to unpack some of the most difficult calculations of the Book of Revelation, Daniel's prophecies, the Exodus of old and the impending Greater Exodus to come, the Temple, the Anti-Christ, the Man of Sin, the False Prophet, The Plagues, The Appointed Times, etc. etc. This Book brings another level to these areas of discussion. The atmosphere has never been so supercharged in our day and ubiquitous with anticipation and even dread regarding these very things. Many are in hopes of escaping the test of the Bride, to simply vanish in thin air from the Tribulation, but to their blindness in part, they will only find themselves walking out what they never thought would happen to them. Judgment, not condemnation, begins in the House of Elohiym.

The nations of planet Earth are in an uproar as if the water pot has been heated up one last time before the outpouring of the Tribulation. There have been countless timelines written by many scholars which have been and are used in Bible Colleges to this very day in order to prepare the Body for what seems to be stirring amongst the nations and prophecy as I write this Foreword. Yet, none seem to connect all the dots to prophetic events that are waiting in the balance, ready to be poured out through His Holy Angels by the Divine hands of the Creator, who sits on the Throne.

As I write this Foreword, I sit in awe and great anticipation for all who are about to read the material concealed in this book. I have heard, I have watched, I have listened and I have read this revelation that has been preached and taught by the Author and willing vessel of this Book. Now, in book form, there are no more excuses to prepare for what is coming! He was poured out himself in order to be found trustworthy by Yeshua to communicate some of the most mind blowing and breathtaking connections I have ever heard from a pulpit and seen from the Hebrew language and pages of Scripture.

The Language of Creation just seems to be a part of this Author's DNA as his continued anointing to unravel the mysteries already seen from several completed works: *The Rainbow Language, The Serpent's Seed, Ezekiel's Wheel Within A Wheel* and now the capstone monument thus far to this priceless library of truth, knowledge, wisdom, revelation and experience used to present to the reader. Now, in Book form, at the fingertips of the reader; "The Plagues of the Greater Exodus" is ready to walk off the pages as the imagination and prophetic unction that will be given as soon as the avid student of Scripture opens up the pages.

You will see why we must stay close to our High Priest and King Yeshua as the Antichrist and Beast system is already at work. You will see powerful connections to the man of sin, the Temple deception, Levitical Hierarchy that will blind the believer if possible, with a strong sacrificial delusion. You will be given the prophetic connections of the Exodus of old and the Greater Exodus already beginning to take formation right before our eyes. I believe the Angels are ready, the vials are full, the Shofar on Heaven's majestic balconies are standing at attention as the time of the Great Tribulation is fast approaching. Do you sense the shift in the atmosphere?

This Book contains so much to talk about for generations to come. The material embedded inside is not to be taken lightly by any means. Whoever you are, you will be challenged, changed and transformed when you read this revelation scribed by the Author. You will understand during this very crucial hour in history, the greatest deception known to mankind is about to be unleashed upon the Religious masses and upon this Earth! The Treasure in the field is about to be redeemed! This is the time and season to buckle up because, we are all about to go for a ride through history and take our final destination into the impending future that awaits us all in the pages of this prophetic work!

Can you smell it in the atmosphere already? Everything seems to be in place as we speak. Heaven has heard the cries of the people. Time seems to be speeding up, so let the prophetic journey begin!

Shepherd John-James Remnant of Truth International
(John-James of the House of Flores.®)

Preface

Dear Reader:

This Book will be the 4th work that I've had the honor to see go to print. Each of the previous books was a seminal work that took me deeper into their subjects than I ever presumed to be able. I would sit at my desk and tremble with excitement as Father revealed layer upon layer of revelation in regard to the contents. This one has been no different!

However, I've taken certain liberties this time that I haven't before and those allowed me to bring together two different perspectives regarding the shape of the vision for this book. First, we challenged much of the conventional ideas relating to the coming Great Tribulation by going back and framing them within the context of their original blueprint – The Exodus Plagues! Second, we took an in-depth and critical look at the latter from a purely Hebraic vantage point. By doing so, we were allowed to see much more than the traditional pictures of those plagues of blood, frogs, lice, etc. In fact, we found that much more was actually visible in the Hebrew text than we had ever seen in the King's English and without doubt, gave us a more specific and detailed view of those sister plagues of Revelation!

I must say, as foreboding as the Exodus plagues were in their former 'traditional' box, they became even more menacing and the thought of another round of similar plagues in Revelation that much more dreadful! Indeed, as we peeled back layer upon layer of prophetic symbolism that had its peculiar ability to reach back and take the message of the Exodus plagues to a new level of horrendous calamity, we saw what was set to befall those who would be 'Coming out of a future Babylon/Egypt'!

In searching through the hidden clues and putting the Eschatological puzzle pieces in their proper place, we also unearthed an even more alarming plot - by whom we have referred to as the "Elite" or the "Powers That Be" - to enslave and destroy the Masses much in the same way as the Pharaoh of Egypt! We have tried to tie each of these twisted plots together in a manner that will give you, the Reader sufficient information, direction and prayerfully, the tenacity to do what you may with it!

I reverently ask that you take your time in reading this book. Measure carefully everything you hear and do your own research. I challenge you to seek Abba ever more intensively as I believe, these plagues to have already begun! If so, they will only intensify and you will either be enslaved further or set free! Our time is short. Let's get started!

David Mathews

Chapter 1

The Plagues of the Great Tribulation: The Exodus Connection!

There is a no more intriguing subject than End-Time prophecy. Regardless of religious affiliation or belief system one has simply to ask his fellow if there is the possibility of judgment, by a Higher Power, falling upon the earth's inhabitants and you will immediately get a response. Though most often it will not be framed within the context of a learned, biblical exegesis. Further, most of the latter that are biblical scholars tend to frame their perspective predicated upon a traditional interpretation based upon the heinous fallacy of what is commonly called the "Rapture".

It is this doctrine steeped in anti-Semitism that is also anti-Torah, which has cultivated an aura of dismissal related to any position that has the Believing Community facing a series of events during what is commonly called The Tribulation! These occurrences foretell of a period of time in our immediate future much like that described by the apocalyptic events known as the Exodus Plagues.

For this reason, ours has been an assignment of a peculiar distinction! We believe that Scripture should interpret Scripture, specifically the Hebrew texts. We have dared to examine the foundations of latter day eschatology (The Study of End-Time Prophecy) through the lens of the Creator's Language – Hebrew and frame them within the context of other biblical patterns and blueprints that are consistent throughout the Scripture.

It is our belief that when one researches the patterns found within Torah you will find they inarguably reveal the methods used by the Creator in delivering Israel from Egypt (Exodus chapters 7-11). Moreover, it naturally follows, since YHVH does not change (Malachi 3:6, Hebrews 13:8) that if a future "Greater Exodus" is to occur, we might just follow that same pattern. That being said, the first 3 plagues fell on both Israel and Egypt alike until finally, in Chapter 8 verses 22 and 23 we find that YHVH makes a distinction between the two Peoples so that the 4th plague – the swarms of flies – doesn't come near their dwellings in Goshen! Why does the Creator intervene here at the 4th plague? We'll answer this later...

To corroborate our position, the Brit Chadashah is replete with hidden connections between these two parallel events: The First Exodus and The Coming Greater Exodus. These hidden connections should serve as tools both to inform and equip the House of Israel for our coming deliverance and the appearance of *our Deliverer*! Let's touch on this for a moment! By the Way, the greater the Exodus, the greater the plagues, the greater the deliverance!

Now, every student of End-Time prophecy spends a fair amount of time expositing the conditions that will produce the arch-type of the above Deliverer – The Anti-Messiah! Further, our Jewish brothers anticipate the appearance of 'their' Messiah in what we would deem a simultaneous spiritual explosion of sorts, much like the "Immovable force meeting the Unstoppable Object". Those of us caught in the middle have an advantage that I hope to exploit here! So, wouldn't you think that recognizing that Deliverer of paramount importance to the Believers?

**Author's note: As of the date of this writing Apr-08-2021 the internet is rife with videos and commentary detailing the events of what was supposedly the unveiling of the Messiah in Israel during Passover! Coincidence? I think not!

Few would argue that the individual cast in the mold of Deliverer depicted in the 1st-Exodus encounter was of course, Moshe (Though he actually represented YHVH)! His name is defined as meaning "One from out of whom the water is drawn". That being said, we should expect the Deliverer of the Greater Exodus to be an identical twin of his, so to speak. Careful now, else your preconceived traditions will catch you unawares!

Will it be Yahshua, the Messiah who arrives bodily to extricate us from the clutches of the Evil One? Again, take care dear Reader. To speak candidly with you, scriptural research leads one to believe that Yahshua arrives on the scene much later –not to lead the Greater Exodus – but, in fact, after the Outcasts have already been gathered and set free! (Psalms 110:1, Matthew 22:44, Mark 12:36, Luke 20:43, Hebrews 1:13, 10:13) WHAT? Who then is the true Deliverer of the Outcasts of Israel in the future Greater Exodus? Are you intrigued enough to continue? Let's delve into this a bit…

Each of the above verses speak of Mashiach sitting at the right hand of YHVH until He – YHVH – makes the enemies of Messiah His footstool! This doesn't fit well in the mold cast by most regarding the 2nd coming of Yahshua! Further, there is no connection to the Church-taught rapture doctrine! We must remember that YHVH does things in the earth *primarily* through people!

Let's Examine the Hebrew Text of Psalms. 110:1

[[A Psalm of David.]] The LORD said unto my Lord, Sit thou at my right hand, until I make thine enemies thy footstool.

- Sit, H#3427   יָשַׁב   Yashav

    Translated as Yashav, and meaning to dwell, remain, and to abide.

If we break the word apart, the Yod prefix indicates 3rd-person future tense, 'He will' - while, the Shin-Bet root produces 'shuv' – to return! Further, Yashav can also connote the 'condition of being married'. Therefore, the Marriage Unit becomes the pattern as the two, man and wife – see Him return or become manifest as they become One! The Yod-Shin root is an adverbial form – how, when, where, why, to what extent, how often, how much – but it points toward possession or property. The Bet indicates the house.

Yashav seems then to point toward the Union of the Bride and her Husband as the point where Messiah becomes Visible or Manifest an event that precedes the property or inheritance of their House being restored!

**Remember, Messiah is the GARMENT OF THE WORD, which Mosheh wore! This 'union' occurs at the moment the Ketubah (A Hebrew word indicating the document displaying the marital vows) is presented, understood and accepted!

The Ketubah being the Torah! After this fashion, the Bride literally 'Puts on' Messiah as a garment! She literally is sanctioned to function in His stead! If this is true, then perhaps it's the Bride out of whom Water shall be drawn in these Last days?

**See John 7:38: *He that believeth on me, as the scripture hath said, out of his belly shall flow rivers of living water.* Let's continue…

In our pursuit of Psalms 110:1 we'll probe a bit deeper into the Hebrew text and look at our next word, in this case the English word is 'right' denoting direction. But the Hebraic text explodes our point of view and allows us to see more of the Mind of the Creator! How so? This word Right, H#3225, ימין, pronounced yamiyn, is traditionally associated with direction, as in the 'right hand'. For emphasis, this is the hand of Covenant and blessing. Incidentally, it is related to the Hebrew word Amen, aman, אמן, meaning to trust, one who produces a skilled work, to agree, faithfulness, full reliability, to bring under one's care, and a pillar or doorpost, signifying a threshold.

This seems to infer that while Yahshua is at 'the Right Hand' of the throne, YHVH has commissioned-endowed another who has proven reliable, trustworthy, and skilled in faithful work and able to bring Creation under the care or across the threshold of His House! Could it be those 'Cloaked in Yahshua – the Messiah – The Word Garment?' Let me point you toward a powerful confirmation!

**See Romans 8:19: *…creation waits for the manifestation of the sons of YHVH.*

Proceeding with our observation of Psalms 110:1 the succeeding word in our translation is the English word 'make' as in to fashion, create, et cetera. However, this is a poor rendering of the Hebrew word used here outlined as: Make, H#7896, שית, pronounced as shiyth, and defined here in its adverbial form – 'until' – however, the same Hebrew letters give us a word specifying a garment!

Further, it is attached to a hyphenated phrase: עד – אשית Ed-'ashiyth. The word 'Ed' is also translated as a conjunction here (until) making its use redundant since shiyth is also rendered, by the translators, as 'until'. However, Ed also indicates 'witness or testimony'. Now, notice the Alef prefixed to shiyth which gives us 3rd-person future tense, 'I will': As we've translated this it could easily read: *"Witness or testify as I will garment (them)"*. Continuing with Psalm 110…

- Enemies, H#341   איב   '*Oyeb*

    This word is translated as enemies: **remember the translators supply punctuation. I believe this should begin a separate definitive statement. The suffixed Kaf supplies ownership – 'your enemies'.

- Thy footstool, H#1916, H#7272,

    from the root רגל הדם

    The translators added the grammatical prefix Lamed (For, to, toward) and suffixes for possession and plurality. *Hadom leragleyka* can literally be translated: 'Your enemies are your footstool'!

Our extrapolated definitions add a new perspective to an amazingly powerful revelation! It seems that Yahshua is depicted as occupying a place in the heavens – The Right Hand of YHVH – [**Thy will be done, on earth as it is in heaven…**] in order that His ambassador on the earth, His Bride may be clothed in His Messianic role as 'The Word' – literally "IN HIM". Further, He is called to witness as YHVH 'Garments her'! This results in the prophetic declaration regarding the end result of her status change – 'Your enemies are (now) your (plural) footstool'! Both Yahshua and the Bride!

As an interesting afterthought, the Ark of the Covenant was considered the footstool of YHVH in the earth (Psalms 132:7), as well as the Altar. Could both the Bride and the enemies of YHVH represent a 'living sacrifice' - one purified while the other is wholly consumed?

Let me call your attention here to this same Psalms 110:4 and the reference to the Melchizedec Order! The Hebrew word for order is H#1700, דִּבְרָה, dibrah, which is rather impotently translated 'order' here. It is the feminine of debar, a word signifying the conceived result of a seed or word released. At the same time, dibrah as a judicial term indicates a 'suit or style, a cause' (A lawful term) as well as an ESTATE!

The latter representing the Standing of the Man and his assets, rights, interests, entitlements, property! *In Civil law the equivalent is patrimony* – the estate created by marriage and shared by spouses! Does this affect our Exodus/Revelation Plague paradigm?

In the interests of clarity, perhaps we should examine the 1st 3 plagues which fell on both Peoples – Israel and Egypt? Of course! Judgment must begin at His House first! His Bride was being prepared. The Greater Exodus reveals this: Rev. 19:7 *Let us be glad and rejoice, and give honour to him: for the marriage of the Lamb is come, and his wife hath made herself ready.* However, for comparison's sake, we must remember that the Book of Revelation is NOT in chronological order!

The First 3 Plagues - Blood-Frogs-Lice: Why Did Israel Have to Experience These?

Exodus 7:17 *Thus saith the YHVH, In this thou shalt know that I am the YHVH: behold, I will smite with the rod that is in mine hand upon the waters which are in the river, and they shall be turned to blood.* **Who Does This Rod Represent?**

Psalms. 110:2 The LORD shall send the rod of thy strength out of Zion: rule thou in the midst of thine enemies.

Interestingly, it seems grammatically that it is YHVH speaking in the 1st-person here! *"I will smite with the rod that is in mine hand..."* Who was this rod? The word used is H#4294, מטה, matteh, which is written במטה, b'matteh - the Bet meaning 'with, in,' etc. Yet, it could also indicate House or Bride! *Remember, we have Moshe-Mashiach and Israel-Bride functioning as a Union! Though matteh can mean a 'rod' it also can indicate a Branch and a Scepter! Are we saying the House/Bride has the Scepter? In our text, Moshe has 'put on' Messiah (Exodus 7:1 *I have made you a god to pharaoh*) and functions as Yahshua in the physical realm!

Is it a stretch of Faith or blasphemous for us to expect the Bride to function in a future Mosaic-Messiah role as well? I think not! Hard Questions get Hard Answers: Why was the plague of Blood the 1st? Will We See These Same Plagues Again and if so, When? Once again for ease of reference and context we'll look at the Hebrew text of Exodus 7:17.

- Blood, H#1818   דם   *Dam*

    The Nile River was said to represent the god of the Dead – Osiris, the Green-Skinned god of the underworld! The Egyptians believed the Nile River was the bloodstream of this deity who is 'reborn' each year! Thus, he was the *Firstborn of many brethren*. This clearly takes us back to Genesis 3 and the need for the shedding of blood for the remission of sin. However, no entity, no man, is sinless and thus, as such, we are incapable of being 'reborn'.

Incidentally, these same letters for blood read backwards Mem-Dalet, מד, give us Mad – another Hebrew word for garment. In this instance it is profoundly evident this was a blood garment rather than a light garment, illustrating an *after the fall* event in typology!

If so, then this 1st plague, a blood plague - seems a call to true repentance and faith in the Shed Blood of Messiah, not that of the blood of bulls and goats which can only set off the penalty for a time and cannot produce a 'born-again' experience! In essence then, the blood plague was a contrast between the Melchizedec Order as a 'living sacrifice' and that of the animal Sacrificial offering of bulls and goats, the offering of which contained NO – spirit, soul – only the Nephesh – and thus, could only postpone the judgment – this issue of blood guiltiness had to be dealt with first!

Israel was about to go into a wilderness journey and with the implementation of the animal sacrifice YHVH had to show them it was only a substitute pattern in and of itself and for that reason could only suffice until the coming of the Living Adam whose righteous blood alone could cleanse! That being said could the Pied Piper-like march toward a 3rd-Temple reinstitution of animal bloodletting produce an almost rabid trust in such a dead work and therefore point back toward this 1st-plague representing bloodshed?

Curiously, the ancient center of Osiris worship was at the place called Abydos, which sounds remarkably like the name of the King of the Pit or Abyss – called Abaddon or Apollyon in the Greek and spoken of in the Book of Revelation! In this context what ancient place, could once again be the location where this PIT is opened? Watch this!

During the plagues Pharaoh's servants make this subtle yet, revealing statement:

The Exodus Keys

Ex. 10:7 *And Pharaoh's servants said unto him, How long shall this man be a snare unto us? Let the men go, that they may serve the LORD their God: knowest thou not yet that Egypt is* **destroyed**?

**NOTE THIS WORD.

- Destroyed, H#6   אבדה   *Avadah*

    This is the same root as Abaddon! Though this word is translated as a verb, it could also be a NOUN – rendering this statement: *Don't you know yet that Egypt is Abaddon?* In fact, it is said that the Ruling Power over Egypt during the 1st Exodus, was in fact this same Abaddon who it is said to have also ruled over Sodom. Making the following note a sobering text.

Note Revelation 11:8 *And their dead bodies shall lie in the street of the great city (Jerusalem), which spiritually is called* **Sodom *and* **Egypt**, *where also our Lord was crucified.*

I find it intriguing that the area in Jerusalem whose ownership is disputed by Jews, Muslims and Christians alike, contains a unique place admitted by all the above as one of their holiest sites: Known as the Dome of the Rock or in Hebrew 'Eben h'Shetiya' – This Foundation Stone is said to sit atop the Center of the World and serves as a cover for the Abyss containing the raging waters of the Flood!

This 1st plague of Blood lasted 7-days – symbolic of 7000 years, at which time the flesh of Man will be restored to the Pre-Edenic condition where the congealed Blood of the flesh becomes Light once again! From the natural, neither Pharaoh and his people, nor the people of Israel could drink of nor wash him or herself in this blood! In practical terms this plague exposed the fallacy of Egypt's misplaced idolatry.

There was/is no life or cleansing in the blood of Osiris! Yet, contrarily, we find Yahshua admonishing His servants to *'eat His flesh and drink His blood'* John 6:52-57 Osiris could not provide this for his worshipers! The life of the flesh is in the Messiah's Blood! As a side note, the mystical god Osiris was said to be linked to the ancient number 7 helping us to understand why this plague lasted 7-days.

In summation here: There is Power in The Blood of Yahshua and consequences to the shedding of the righteous blood of His People and the World will see that Power!

> Revelation 16:6 *For they have shed the blood of saints and prophets, and thou hast given them blood to drink; for they are worthy.*

The 1st Plague: Blood[1]

---
[1] Sabine Alex http://www.torah-illustrations.blogspot.com/
Used with permission.

Chapter 2

The Plague of Frogs

For most, the KJV gives a satisfactory description of these plagues. The Reader glosses over the text and seldom delves any deeper than the surface. In contrast, by now you must've realized that we are diligent in excavating the Truth where it is more often than not, hidden in the bedrock of the Hebrew text. Take this next plague – Frogs. Is it possible, though it is quite dreadful as simply a reptilian scourge, that there is a far more sinister plot that bodes a terrible future to those who will experience this 2nd plague in the near future? Take a peek in the depths of the Hebrew language and see for yourself!

- Frogs, H#6854   צפרדע   *Tsephardea*

    This word is rendered frogs here, but is related to tsafar, to go in a circle, revolve, or leap in a dance, to pip or chirp as a bird.

It also hints at leaving, a departure of sorts. The 2-end letters Dalet-Ayin give us the word for 'knowledge'. It is also used to mean 'a swamp'. (Perhaps draining the swamp takes on new meaning?)

This is a powerful root – Dalet-Ayin, first seen in Genesis. 2:9

where the Etz H'da'at, the Tree of knowledge of good and evil is first seen. Da'at is the knowledge of 'ME' – Self. Reversing the letters – Ayin-Dalet, `Ed – gives us witness or testimony. The numeric value (74) Ayin = 70, Dalet = 4 is the same as the Hebrew name for Esther - Hadassah, to hide, cover.

Etz H'da'at has a gematria of 645, the same as עֵין הַתַּנִּין, Ayin h`taniyn – translated as Dragon's Well which was the area discussed in Nehemiah 2:13. It is my opinion that the Temple stood 100's of yards from the supposed Temple Mount known by most today! The Greek Septuagint reads *'pege ton sukon'* the fountain of the figs. Could this have been where Adam and Chavah (Eve) covered themselves with fig leaves after eating from the above Tree of Knowledge?

As we examine our extrapolated definition what we're seeing are more than merely frog invasions! In fact, it seems a calculated stratagem by the Most High to release this blight upon both Israel and Egypt for an express purpose. What you ask?

This plague exposes or uncovers the hidden 'god of Self'. The 'leaving of the knowledge of the Tree of Life for that of the Tree of Knowledge is implied.' Moral or Torah standards are no longer the compass of direction for man's righteous boundaries! The Sages teach da`at is related to the development of language and one who lacks Torah knowledge, i.e. is governed by SELF, is akin to an 'untrained deaf mute' having no mind of their own! It seems both Nations suffered from this malady!

Curiously, this is the only plague in which Moshe cried out for YHVH to remove!

> Exodus 8:12 ... *and Moses* **cried** *unto the LORD* **because** *of the frogs...*

**Note the highlighted words! Now, why would those words be hidden there?

The Exodus Keys

The word for Cried out is H#6817, צעק, tzoak, to cry out, make an outcry. It is the same two-letter root, Tzade-Qof as Isaac – to make sport, make fun of! The word 'because' is H#1697, דָּבָר, Dabar, defined as word, utterance, saying, speaking! What are the frogs known for, but their incessant, unintelligible, 'speaking'! Could Moshe have been ridiculing the 'words' of these frog 'gods' for their inability to communicate 'croak' deliverance to their worshippers? Perhaps a bit of sarcasm such as Elijah displayed?

The Future Frog Fracas!

The 2nd Plague: Frogs[#2]

Most scholars agree the frogs represented the ancient goddess of childbirth, Heket, known as the goddess of birthing - midwifery –

[#2] Sabine Alex http://www.torah-illustrations.blogspot.com/
Used with permission.

she chose the child's gender emphasizing who would live and indeed has been depicted as representing a tribal matriarchal society, where males are emasculated or diminished! Anthropomorphic (Attributing human traits to animals or non-humans, hybrids such as Nephylim, and AI – artificial intelligence) She was also venerated at Abydos – as was Osiris!

Now we can make the connection found in Exodus 1:15 where Pharaoh solicited the 'Midwives' of the Hebrews to kill the unborn male children! The etymological connection between צפרדע, Tsephardea and one of the Midwives of the Hebrew women - שִׁפְרָה, Shiphrah (a clear, vibrant, brightness, splendid, to adorn) is uncanny and intriguing - both contain a cognate root Tzade-Pey-Resh, Shin-Pey-Resh, which is striking! *Midrash Tadshe, Ozar Ha-Midrashim, [Eisenstein, p.474]* infers that Shiphrah was not Hebrew, but a pious, Egyptian![#3] (Quite possibly, a Heket convert in my opinion). In addition to the above connection, the name of Moshe's wife also comes to mind – H#6855, צִפֹּרָה, Zipporah, which originates from the same root – Tzade-Pey-Resh, tsaphar indicating to leap or dance in a circle, to chirp or twitter! Each of these words confuses the translators, yet a link to Shophar, as in a trumpet, which gives a clear, distinct 'covering of sound', binds each definition together!

Could there be another End-Times scenario that will follow the Exodus Pattern and thus, a future Pharaoh who compels Heket's consorts, those who would attempt to manipulate the population through various birth control methods, such as abortion, and with such genetic modifications as those revealed as having already been prepared for use in the mass extermination of a large part of the populace through forced vaccination, Electro-Magnetic-Frequencies, 5G technology and much more in order to destroy, by making sterile - the Men in the earth in an effort to control the appearance of the Man – Messiah? It happened in Moshe's day, it

---

[#3] *Midrash Tadshe, Ozar Ha-Midrashim, [Eisenstein, p.474]* for attribution purposes. No direct quote.

happened again in Yahshua's day and it will/is happening now!

Revelation 16:13 indicates a season when unclean spirits *like frogs* issue forth out of the mouth of the dragon, the beast and the false prophet! Those who hearken to their voices will assemble to the battle of Armageddon and destruction! We will consider the latter in depth as we look at what I like to call the 11th Plague – The Red Sea Crossing. We will reserve that for the conclusion of this book!

For now, as we complete our look at the Plague of Frogs I found an interesting bit of intelligence material packaged in one of the elaborate schemes of the Elites who would control the information that is disseminated through all social media platforms. In 2015 an online image board called '4chan' an Internet subculture began posting a Frog Meme connected to Donald Trump, giving the frog the Korean name 'Kek' (a croaking laugh in substitute for LOL - laugh out loud) and users started making the Heket connection.

As of today's date: April 13th 2021 many of the Leaders in Mainstream conservatism and in particular the Religious Community seemed to echo the seductive Croak and untruthful disinformation of the Frogs reminiscent of those same Lying Frogs of Revelation as they, along with the Messianic and Hebrew Roots Believers began to tout the Trump administration as the Redeemer of America! How ironic those Believers who purportedly hear from the Creator seemed all too content to have 'One more night with the Frogs' as did Pharaoh!

The above 2 previous plagues saw the Egyptian Sorcerers being able to duplicate them. Just as the Powers That Be in the above illustrations during the Greater Exodus Plagues. However, this 3rd plague presented the Magicians of Pharaoh with a new twist.

The 3rd Plague: Lice[#4]

It is possible that most students of End-Times Prophecy and what is commonly called "The Tribulation Period" have failed to distinguish between the Wrath of Satan and the Wrath of YHVH! If the "Sorcerers of Modern Babylon-Egypt" like those ancient Magicians, fail to duplicate the coming Plague of Lice; perhaps the "Finger of YHVH" is once again being revealed and judgment – His judgment – inescapable! Before us lies the text of Exodus. Be prepared to have your traditional religious paradigms tested!

> Exodus 8:16 *And the LORD said unto Moses, Say unto Aaron, Stretch out thy rod, and smite the dust of the land, that it may become lice throughout all the land of Egypt.*

[#4] Sabine Alex http://www.torah-illustrations.blogspot.com/
Used with permission.

The origin of this plague is seen as the Aaron's rod, the Hebrew is: Matteh – Rod and mentioned early on in our teaching, strikes the 'Dust' – H#6083, עפר, aphar, rendered dry earth, it is contrasted with a word the KJV translators also render as earth, ground. Yet, the Hebrew etymology expounds upon the difference between dust and ground. Consider this word H#127 אֲדָמָה, Adamah, the source from which Adam was created and the word dust – aphar that seems to indicate their Post-fall bodies now absent the Light.

The gematria of aphar is 350 while Adamah is 50, the balance of 300 gives us the value of Kopher – to cover, pitch, make atonement, to forgive! Genesis 3:19 reminds us, though we were taken out of the Adamah, that from the fall until our resurrection we are dust – Aphar – and to dust shall we return or belong. While in this 'aphar' state, we must have someone or something to cover or make atonement for us!

The Genesis text says Adam was *'taken'* from this 'aphar', which in itself begs our indulgence as the English rendering does little to add clarity other than simply removed or made or brought out of something.

I'll take a short aside here to explain what I mean. This English word 'Taken' is from H#3947, לקח, laqach, to take for oneself as in marriage. While in the condition of Adamah – they (Adam and Chavah – Eve) were married, Echad, One with Messiah.

The next phrase in Genesis 3:19 actually shows a specific time period: *For out of it thou was taken* – or until thou was taken – The Hebrew gives us כי-עפר Ki-Aphar. Yet prefixed word Ki also indicates to be burned, scarred, to be branded. Until they became 'branded' the result of which, caused them to return to the dust (who owns them) until kophered – Covered, Ransomed or atoned for! The gematria of Ki-Aphar is 380, the same as מִצְרַיִם, Mitsrayim – Egypt!

As we move forward looking at this enigmatic next Plague, prayerfully what we just shared regarding the 'dust' will help to connect the dots a bit more for you.

The word for Lice here in Exodus 8:16 is H#3654, כן, ken, rendered 'gnats' from the root kanan, a root, support or shoot, stock of a tree. It indicates to cover or protect, to defend. Further, this 3rd-plague is said by the historians to have affected, by the Creator's design, the Egyptian deity known as GEB – the god of the Earth – DUST! This plague was a legal maneuver - on behalf of Israel – by YHVH to get them to agree to remove their selves from the lineage-stock-heritage-protection of the god of the Earth – Satan and seek restoration with YHVH!

In response to their inability to counter this attack, the Egyptian Magicians called this the Finger of god! Finger, in Hebrew is H#676, אצבע 'etsba, finger. However, it comes from the root tseh'vah, meaning to dip, drench, immerse into LIVING WATER! This word is related to Teshuvah – to repent and return!

Could this indicate a ritual Mikveh water immersion - necessary for the Bride to cleanse herself much like at Mt. Sinai in order to wash the dust from her? Further, Geb was known as a 'healing god' and ancient texts do in fact, point to his ability to heal scorpion stings! Please note the future Scorpions of the Greater Exodus Plagues shown in Revelation. 9:3,4,5:

> *And there came out of the smoke locusts upon the earth: and unto them was given power, as the scorpions of the earth have power. And it was commanded them that they should not hurt the grass of the earth, neither any green thing, neither any tree; but only those men which have not the seal of God in their foreheads. And to them it was given that they should not kill them, but that they should be tormented five months: and their torment was as the torment of a scorpion, when he striketh a man.*

As we've stated previously, during our in-depth look into the 1st 3-Exodus plagues and our explanation for the reasons they fell upon both Israel and Egypt alike, it has become painfully evident that Israel must have been in a backslidden condition and had gradually incorporated the pagan idolatrous practices of Egypt's religion into their own.

Thus, YHVH had to remind them of the Promised Seed, the Shedding of blood for the remission of sins, and the need for a return to the Faith of their Fathers! This sounds exactly like the condition of today's Believing community as a whole and if judgment begins at His House first, then we can expect and we must prepare for, the blood, frogs and lice that are arriving now!

Sadly, as we contemplate our future, most Believers are not preparing for a tribulation lifestyle much less, the anticipation of an even Greater Exodus as the Outcasts of Israel are currently being gathered from the 4-corners of the world. You would think that serious bible scholars would want pertinent information and that given the opportunity, they would quickly develop the attitude of 2Timothy 2:15 wherein we're admonished to *'rightly divide the word of Truth'* rather than allow ourselves to be made ashamed. What dear Reader could possibly happen to bring shame upon such an august body as those who call themselves Believers?

Is it possible that we've been intentionally mislead by false teachings and false doctrines that leave us wholly unprepared for this End-Times event called 'Tribulation'? I firmly believe so! In fact, one of the most damnable doctrines is that of the RAPTURE! The idea that all those 'Christians' will somehow escape any tribulation wrath, a judgment that is somehow reserved for those rebellious unbelievers left behind and of course, the Jews is simply ludicrous! Frankly, this smacks of an anti-Torah and an anti-Semitic bias that can only serve to alienate any possibility of a Union of the House of Judah and the House of Ephraim or Israel, which is inherently comprised of those of the dispersal who find themselves immersed in the Nations! But, what about the next plagues: How, when and to what extent will Israel, which include those believing Christians, endure, much less survive them?

The Land of Goshen

After judging His House during the 1st-3 plagues, a People that in our Exodus text, are currently residing in Goshen, YHVH now makes a proclamation:

> Exodus 8:22,23 *And I will sever in that day the land of Goshen, in which my people dwell, that no swarms of flies shall be there; to the end thou mayest know that I am the LORD in the midst of the earth. And I will put a division between my people and thy people: tomorrow shall this sign be.*

I contend that an explanation of the Name Goshen is pertinent to our study. Oddly enough, it has been a source of consternation for many as no Hebrew word supports its use and, further, the fact that a translation argument exists between the Masoretic and Septuagint texts! The former being culpable in numerous translation errors! The Masorets supplied the current KJV English - Goshen, H#1657, גשן, while the Septuagint has Geshem, גשם, and infers that Geshem was situated in Arabia, outside the borders of Egypt proper. Genesis 45:10 (LXX). In borrowing from the ancient work entitled: *The Monthly Review" 1796, George Edward Griffiths, P. 189*[#5] it seems the etymologists of that day felt Goshen derived from a combination of Arabic indicating 'a tongue' and a related Arabic word akin to the Hebrew word מטר, matar, indicating rain or copious springs, wells.

[#5] *"The Monthly Review" 1796, George Edward Griffiths, P. 189* for attribution only. No direct quote.

In fact, the word Geshem in Hebrew indicates rain. The resulting interpretation would give Goshen a connection to the living water or language or tongue of the Hebrews! Goshen has the same gematria as H#4888, mishchah, derived from the same root Mashach (Mashiach-Messiah) to anoint or consecrate, The Anointed One! Since only 70+ original Hebrews first occupied Goshen, and no prior place name existed, it is my opinion that the place *'became known as'* Goshen/Geshem as a result of those Hebrews speaking the Living Waters of the Language of Hebrew, in Goshen, the place of anointing!

Ironically, as we see the plagues arriving on the world's scene today, that same Living Language/Tongue is also being restored. Zephaniah 3:9 calls it a 'pure', H#1305, ברר, barar, to purify, select, but also to sever, separate – language, H#8193, שפה, saphah, language, tongue, lip or border! Accordingly, the Hebrew Tongue separated Goshen/Geshem from Egypt proper! Much like the earth was divided in Peleg's day in Genesis 10.

It is this Hebrew language that will later separate the People of YHVH from Egypt allowing them to serve Him with one consent: לעבדו שכם אחד le'avado shekem `Echad. Please note the root seen as 'serve' – avad, is also the root of the Name of the Fallen Angel who is referred to as the King of the Pit – Abaddon, he who we mentioned in our first part of this study, leading an army whose hordes will torment all those men not separated/marked upon their foreheads as belonging to YHVH!

The phrase above *le'avado shekem Echad* has a value of 485, the same as: תכסה, tikiceh a phrase meaning 'you shall cover or hide'. It could also indicate 'You shall sit on the Throne'! Consequently, it is entirely possible the Language of Creation, the Language of Torah, could in all good conscience, be the instrument of "Marking or Sealing" used to fence off, cover or hide the People of YHVH from those whom Abaddon might attack!

If you'll allow, I want to call your attention once more to the verse cited above: Again, this verse references Abaddon, King of the Pit and his hordes, as seen in Revelation 9:4 *And it was commanded them that they should not hurt the grass of the earth, neither any green thing, neither any tree; but only those men which have not the* **seal** *of God in their* **foreheads**.

Not surprisingly, the Septuagint reveals both of these Greek words which, by their very nature, are connected to their Hebrew counterparts seen in Exodus 28:11,38.

**Please note the following.

- Seal, H#2368   חותם   *Chotham*

  A signet used for identification. To seal up something as a means of protection.

- Forehead, H#4696   מצח   *Metsach*

  The brow or forehead; that which is clear, conspicuous. The Mem-Tzade root is seen in multiple roots that indicate a garrison, outpost, army, a standing monument stone, stronghold, etc. It has the same gematria – 138 – as nephach – to breathe into, release breath.

If we understand the Hebrew letters as individual word pictures, then one should not be surprised as we rearrange them that these same letters give us another powerful Hebrew word: צמח, Tzemach, describing a branch, to spring forth or sprout! This Branch could indicate either the Root or Stem of the Tree of Life, or that of the Tree of Carnal Knowledge! Depending on which seed or breath/word one inhales!

While here, it should be pointed out that Metsach - מצח also has the same letters as חמץ, Chametz – indicating Leaven. Let's spend a few moments understanding how Chametz fits into the context of what we're positing. Most Believers have a skewed perspective regarding Chametz and its prohibition during Pesach, yet, Chametz is embraced on other Holy days including Sabbath, where a 'Raised' loaf is offered. What's the difference and what does Chametz have to do with the sealing of YHVH's people?

Leaven is the agent that puffs up, elevating the flesh, hinting at making it live. No man's flesh should be exalted after this fashion because death works in all, except Messiah Yahshua who warned of the *"leaven of the Pharisees"*: Which was seemingly an indictment of their lifestyle where their religious works, displayed publicly, tended to exalt their office or the individual rather than displaying the attitude of a humbled heart!

I propose this is the reason for the prohibition of Chametz being limited to the Month of Aries, the Lamb – during Pesach! After our Messiah Yahshua is executed or lifted up – Chametz becomes a symbol of the Power of His life to lift the Body out of the grave! In keeping with that, we surmise that only those who lift up Messiah by demonstrating Him in their lives will be 'Marked' or Sealed against the schemes of the King of the Pit! How can I lift Him up one may ask? By speaking, breathing, and releasing His word!

In addition, it is worthwhile to mention that the Levitical system and the implementation of the 3rd Temple sacrificial system, will be a return to the *"leavening of the Pharisees"* and the sanctioning of which will invite a misplaced trust in a system where CHAMETZ – FLESH will once again be offered, yet it cannot be received – whether it's the body of an animal or a man – outside or in lieu of, the BODY of Messiah! Please note the following confirming verses.

1Corinthians 15:50 *Now this I say, brethren, that flesh and blood cannot inherit the kingdom of God; neither doth corruption inherit incorruption.*

Yet again the devices of the KJV translators set us upon and it gives us little room with which to fully understand what the Apostle Paul (Who is the greatest Torah scholar of all Yahshua's converts) is trying to convey. This misunderstanding of the Pauline epistles has led to gross misinterpretations in more places than I have the time to write. Here though, we'll look at the Greek Text and extract the truth for you!

- Flesh, Gk. #4561   *Sarx*

    Flesh, yet this word originates from iro, meaning to raise, elevate, and to lift up! The Chametz-sarx or flesh of the animals or the fallen – corrupt flesh of man cannot give access to the Kingdom!

- Inherit, Gk. #2816   *Klaronomeo*

    This is a compound word from Kleros, indicating to inherit by Son ship and Nomos, the Greek word for Torah! Simply stated, what we can now extract from this verse is powerful to say the least!

THE TORAH DOES NOT PROVIDE A SONSHIP INHERITANCE THROUGH THE FLESH OF ANIMALS OR A FALLEN MAN! ONLY THROUGH MESSIAH!

For Talmudic evidence in support of what we're saying about corrupt flesh (whether animal or man) being suitable for sacrifice, one need only look at their own ancient sources. For example, the Jews felt the Temple was corrupted, or 'destroyed' when anyone defiled or in the slightest degree, damaged anything in it, or if its guardians neglected their duties. (*Deyling, Observv. Sacrae, vol.ii. p. 505sqq*)[#6]

The startling consequence of which, calls attention to the 2nd Temple Period and for that matter, this final 3rd Temple and the notable absence of the Ark of the Covenant which housed the Presence of Elohiym from each Temple, the result of which, rendered it then and now - corrupt, defiled and subject to destruction.

The noun form of this word destruction points to none other than one known as: 'The Destroyer – ABADDON'. For the record let me state that the Adamic flesh itself is a defiled temple.

Now, you know why Yahshua made the statement: Destroy this temple and in 3-days I will raise it up! Speaking of His body, which literally represented the Temple of YHVH on the Earth! In support of their own Oral Traditions He had to destroy the 'corrupted temple body' containing Adam's DNA! 1Corinthians 15:50.

As we digest this info, an enigma presents itself when we consider this "Marking of the Forehead" and it sounds as if the 'forehead' is a strategic part of the Body that Abba specifically targets for protection against the King of the Pit – Abaddon and cannot be relegated to a simple "Mark" or tattooed "666" as most interpret. How so?

It goes without saying, no man can stand against a fallen angelic or demonic power in his flesh alone, and any quote "Mark" that supposedly protects outside of what is prescribed here, is witchcraft! Further, a simple mark would be for identification purposes only! Indeed there must be more to this! Since it identifies us, could this mark actually indicate the condition

---

[#6] (*Deyling, Observv. Sacrae*, vol.ii. p. 505sqq). For attribution only. No direct quote.

whereby the recipients have renewed their minds that we may appropriate the Power of Elohiym, rather than the arm of the flesh!

As we continue, looking once again at Metsach and Chametz which have a value of 138, the same as H#2610, חנף, haneph, to defile, to profane, hypocrisy, and filthiness, to be godless. There seems to be a direct correlation between those who espouse the filthiness and godlessness above versus those who have their minds renewed and walks not according to the flesh. Abaddon will target both, yet only the latter have a personal Goshen, a hiding place in Messiah!

Why? What connection does the Forehead, and a potential "Mark" as a means of protection by YHVH have to do with Goshen/Geshem? Let's take a forensic look into the subject. The forehead is located directly outside the frontal lobe or frontal cortex of the brain. This area controls the cognitive skills of emotional expression, problem solving, and memory, LANGUAGE, judgment and conscience! Whoever controls or "Marks as owned" the forehead controls the Man!

Ironically, one of the surest, easiest ways to affect the frontal lobe is with EMF, such as cell phones, 5G (and the coming 6G 6gimmel 6x3=666) technologies, etc.

Addiction expert Nicholas Kardaras has said after having worked with hundreds of heroin addicts and other hallucinogenic addicts that it is easier to treat either of those than it is to handle the neurosis of a 'Screen Addict'.[7] These latter addicts become severely impaired in areas of impulsivity and decision-making! You connect the dots with the coming assault from the King of the Pit!

---

[7] *Dr. Nicholas Kardaras Ivy-League educated psychologist.* For attribution only. No direct quote.

It is my opinion that Abba has restored the Hebrew language for those looking for a Goshen, as such; the MIND becomes the spiritual safe haven and place of protection. Now, let's continue to look back at the key words of Exodus 8:22,23. Severed and Divided:

The text in Exodus makes 2 things abundantly clear: Number 1 – *YHVH did something special regarding the land of Goshen/ Geshem* by severing it from Egypt at this 4th plague and Number 2 – He put a division between the Peoples as well! Let's look at these two words:

- Sever, H#6395　פלה　*Palah*

    Pronounced palah, this words indicates to make a marvelous and illustrious distinction between something. Its root is related to wonderful, incomprehensible, and miraculous. It hints at creating a watercourse or cleaving a channel, figuratively pointing to a man's fertility or vigor, his being a 'well of offspring'. This word is used in the distinction made between Goshen/Geshem and Egypt! Hearing this, I would think everyone would want to live in Goshen!

- Division, H#6304　פדות　*Peduwth*

    Rendered peduwth; this word is also translated as a distinction, deliverance, redemption and a ransom! Its root is the same as Padah, from whence we get *pidyon ha'ben*, the redemption of the first-born. The word focuses on the Price paid for the ransom, not just the concept of being ransomed!

The usage in both words of the Hebrew letter 'Pey' is not lost on those who are observant. Pey hints at 'mouth, speech, language'. It is highly probable that any deliverance or ransom, i.e. "the sealing on the forehead" – though bought and paid for by Messiah Yahshua – has to be appropriated through SPEAKING! Word's are literally life and/or death. Let's continue...

There seems both a powerful reference calling attention to the Land being 'ransomed and redeemed' as well as, the People.

**Note: 2Chronicles 7:14 *If my people, which are called by my name, shall humble themselves, and pray, and seek my face, and turn from their wicked ways; then will I hear from heaven, and will forgive their sin, and will heal their land*-ארץ.

Throughout the Creation Account an enigma exists between the terms Eretz and Adamah. But, both are translated as land, earth or ground. However, it seems both serve as a euphemistic reference to the BODY of Adam! Eretz being the 'Image' of Elohiym – The Man-Adam out of whom the Woman-Adamah would later be taken!

The root of Eretz – ארץ, Resh-Tzade points toward two powerful words: Ratz, a bar or piece of Silver, and ratzatz, to bruise, or crush! The Alef prefix indicates "I Will". Against this background, the Sod (Deepest, mystical) level of Eretz could be interpreted as *"I Will, as Silver – Keceph (Silver, pale as in color, to be made a shame, take on shame) be bruised, taking on shame in order to ransom!* The Eretz-Earth-Creation became Tohu V'bohu – taking on shame waiting for the Adam to ransom it!

Perhaps you understand Romans 8:19-22 a little better? *For the creature was made subject to vanity, not willingly, but by reason of him who hath subjected the same in hope, because the creature itself also shall be delivered from the bondage of corruption into the glorious liberty of the children of God. For we know that the whole creation groaneth and travaileth in pain together until now.*

To add additional intrigue, Silver - Keceph, H#3701, כסף, has a value of 120, the number of Man's years upon the earth, as well as, the number of Jubilee's assigned to the earth's season of exile or Tohu V'bohu condition (50x120=6000) and is also the value of the word Mo'ed, an appointed place, time or signal: A festival season. Ironically, the Mem prefix of Mo'ed indicates a 'womb', while its root, Yod-Ayin-Dalet, ya'ad, hints at 'espousing a wife'. The Adam had to take a wife in order to conceive, womb and birth the ransom! What promises have you conceived, wombed and are waiting to birth?

That number 120 is also the value of מסך, masak, and the word indicating the Covering or Veil that was rent in the Temple upon the Execution of Messiah! This tearing of the veil represented the renting/bruising of the Last Adam's flesh (Yahshua) as He prepared the Way for all men to return to YHVH! This was a prophetic glimpse inside of Creation where that which had once become Tohu V'bohu – along with Adam and Eve-Chavah, who themselves were the spiritual Tent of the Congregation – Ohel Mow'ed – would see the One Who Would Ransom birthed (Yahshua the Last Adam) who would reverse the curse! The Wilderness Tabernacle with its animal sacrifice was a shadow picture of that same Tohu V'bohu world, waiting for the coming of the MAN – That Last Adam – who would set Creation Free!

As living Practice for the Real Act, each of the Moedim - are rehearsals and as such, a living Screenplay where we come to prepare for the final act of Redemption of both Eretz and the Body!

It is my position that this ransom process began in Genesis 1, and continued through chapter 2 where YHVH formed a Body out of the ADAMAH and bruising the flesh of the Elohiym-Image Adam, took the Ishah out of him in order to expedite the redemption of Creation! Adamah has a value of 50, the same as YOVEL – the Hebrew word meaning Jubilee or release. *The Adamah was the source of Jubilee, release, and a return from Tohu V'bohu – waste and desolation!*

This helps explain the distinction made between the Flesh/Land-Eretz of Goshen that has been 'Redeemed' by/through the Blood of the 1st 3-plagues and the Carnal land of Egypt – the flesh which must be judged! Straightaway, there now remains a severing of the people themselves who must be 'taken out of the carnal Tohu V'bohu body' – the land of Egypt! The word for 'my people' is עמי, ami, which with a value of 120 again connects us to the aforementioned Hebrew word H#4539 מסך, masak, the curtain or veil in the Temple that was torn!

Do you see what is happening? This is only at the beginning of the 4th plague! The number 4 is written with the Dalet – The Door! These 10 plagues follow Creation's history, restoring what was Fallen, that which was without form and void, to its original state! Israel was supposed to be the Collective ADAM!

The 10th plague is that which deals with the death of the First-Born or Ransom of the First-Born! What's being said? YHVH caused a Boundary to be established between the Land of Israel and that of Egypt. He follows the Genesis creation pattern in reverse: restoring – judging the man/Israel/Egypt first, and restoring – judging the animals/land/earth in the following plagues! We will see this same pattern play out in the final scenes of the infamous Tribulation Period! Abba is preparing you dear Reader to 'come out of her My People'!

As we continue, the word for land, H#776, ארץ, 'Eretz is the 7th word of Torah – Genesis 1:1 where inside the word 'Eretz, we see revealed the 26th, 27th and 28th letters of the written Torah. 26 is the value of YHVH and Kavod-Glory, weighty or splendor. 27 is the value of Chiydah – a riddle, an enigma, a proverb, an oracle or vision that is hidden. 28 is the value of Koah, indicating power, strength and might! Their combined value is 81, the gematria of Kiceh – Throne and Avodah – service, which, notably, is also the root of Abaddon!

The letters of 'Eretz and their numeric values reveal a previously hidden oracle, wherein the Earth – Eretz, is witness to the Vision, Power, and Strength of Elohiym and His throne and those who serve Him contrasted with those who will bow to the Destroyer – Abaddon!

It seems the 1st – 3rd plagues had more to do with redeeming the People/Adam while the 4th – 10th would enable/empower them to set free the Land – Eretz! This is what we're expecting now – an empowering of the People, as the Tohu V'bohu – flesh is conquered and Creation awaits the Manifestation of the Sons of Elohiym!

> Romans 8:19 *For the earnest expectation of the creature waiteth for the manifestation of the sons of God.*

Chapter 3

The 4th Plague: Swarms of Flies[#8]

To begin here, I want you to note that the word 'flies' is in italics and supplied by the translators not being in the original text. Conventional translators are divided on the meaning of the word preceding 'flies' which is an interesting Hebrew word not

---

[#8] Sabine Alex http://www.torah-illustrations.blogspot.com/
Used with permission.

necessarily indicating flying insects; the KJV word is: – *swarm*, while the Hebrew has H#6157, ערב; pronounced 'Arob; which is here translated as a swarm, mingled, a mixture, incessant. It comes from 'Arab, to pledge, exchange to become surety or to exchange articles of traffic, to barter and to interweave.

The controversy surrounding the writer's choice of 'Arob is unsettling. Scholars are divided regarding its meaning with some declaring a flying – swarming group of insects, while others a group of marauding animals. The most disturbing head scratching seems centered around verse 31 ...*there remained not one*. After the plague is over how could not even one insect have been found out of the *millions* required for a 'swarm'? Here is where unconventional thinking requires one to set aside his religious traditions and do a bit of detective work if you want to truly get to the bottom of this controversy!

By word of Caution! Those same letters rearranged give us עבר - EBER – the root word indicating to cross over, as in to gain one's inheritance/promised land and also, to stand opposite of or in opposition to. In EBER son's day the Earth was divided - Peleg!

These Swarms are about to be unleashed as the 4th plague – the Door to the Pit is opened. Who will stand in opposition to them?

FYI: Eber is seen in Genesis 10:25 yet; verse 9 tells us of Nimrod who initiates the Tower of BABEL – The language of Mystery! Perhaps a key to opposing these swarms is found in the knowledge gleaned from the Hebrew language. In that regard, it is from the name Eber that we get the word Hebrew or Ivrit. In his capacity as a carrier of the language of Creation Eber was able to stand in opposition to Nimrod whose name incidentally, has a value of 294, while Eber is 272, the difference? 22, the number of Hebrew letters! Coincidence? You make the call!

David Mathews

Who Are These Swarms?
An Ancient Extra-Biblical Clue

Exodus 8:15,19,32 ...*And Pharaoh hardened his heart*: את-לבּו ויכבד פרעה *Ve'yachved par`oh Et-livo*. The key root is Kavod, indicating a heavy heart. In the ancient Egyptian Book of the Dead, a deceased person's heart is revealed as being weighed against a feather. The god Anubis, who guards passage into the underworld by determining if the heart is lighter than the feather, oversees the scales or balance weighing the heart.

It seems Moshe is familiar with the Book of the Dead and Pharaoh is being told his wickedness has caused his heart to be Kavod – heavy and judgment waits!

According to Egyptian mythology,[#9] as punishment for such a wicked one, Ammit, the Devourer of Hearts or Soul Eater, would swallow the heart of the offender who would be consigned to eternal restlessness and would die the 2nd death! Ancient Egyptians feared this god Ammit, the heart eater greatly!

Here is where a connection to the 4th plague seems likely! Ammit or Ammut as an Egyptian god was a hybrid chimera-type Nephylim with the head of a crocodile (Some believe a Dragon) the body of a lion and the rear of a hippo. Each of these animals, especially if 'swarms' of a combination of each overran Egypt, would have brought unspeakable terror upon its inhabitants!

Further, `Arob is etymologically related to Erev, meaning evening, darkness and coupled with the horror of the menacing animals above provided an intense terror not felt prior! *Note the words of the Psalmist regarding this incident!

Psalms 78:45 *He sent divers sorts of flies -* `*arob - among*

[#9] https://en.wikipedia.org/wiki/Ammit For attribution only. No direct quote.

> *them, which devoured –akal, to eat, feed upon - them; and frogs, which destroyed them.*

If I read this correctly, as incredulous as it may seem, it looks as if the Swarms ate, devoured or consumed the Egyptians!

It is worth noting that most occultists include the above description within the overall characteristics of what most would describe as the mythical, supernatural dragon.

Here, I want to leap forward again to Revelation 9:3-11 where the flying 'scorpion-like' locusts (Dragons?) are sent to torment those not sealed by YHVH. There is a powerful link found here connecting us once again, to the AROV-SWARMS. However, it confirms our suspicion that these entities are far more than a scourge of insects. Please note The Greek word for scorpion, G#4651, skorpios which is taken from G#4649, skopos, translated as a watchman, a concealed sentry or spy, and related to skepasma, a covering. These "Beings" or "Swarms' in my opinion, have a different fleshly garment, i.e. they seem to be Fallen Ones, Nephylim or Watchers! The Hebrew equivalent to this Greek name is עקרב, Akrab, very similar to `arov, and also indicates conflict or war.

Thus begs the question: Is the Abyss about to open and unleash these 'Beings' – the Greater Swarm of the Greater Exodus upon Egypt, i.e. the World/Whirled – those caught in the tornado of Oz? This last statement may confuse the Reader. However, take a few hours and go back and watch the old Wizard of Oz movie. This time, pray for understanding that your eyes are opened. You will begin to see the Plans of the Elite are unfolding just as they 'magically' revealed through their witch-like enchantments and have been for several generations! Thus, it becomes imperative for the Reader to rightly divide the word of truth, else fall prey to the seductions of our common enemy! Let's continue…

These Swarms, I prefer Scorpions or dragons, torment men for 5-

months: 5x30 = 150 days, the same length of time Noah's floodwaters were upon the earth. During this period of torment or judgment, YHVH tells Noah the entirety of those not inside the ARK – Goshen – during the Geshem-Rain, deluge will be destroyed! Yet, He will establish His Covenant with Noah – ensuring those inside the Ark will not be hurt. The word for Ark, H#8392, תבה, teviah, has a value of 407, the same as: אות, owth, a sign – MARK.

To make it plain for you, a mark received outside of Goshen, the protected place, subjects one to the control or mark of the Dragon! Please look at the confirmation found in the numeric values of Teviah – Ark = 407 – Goshen = 353 = 54. 9x6 or 666666666!

In parallel to the part about the Egyptian gods Ammit and Anubis, another affirmation of our position would be that of the Ancient Zodiacal Prophecies of the Signs which foretell in advance, every major event regarding the Redemptive plan of the Creator. As those signs would change each 2160 years their testimony or 'witness' as Genesis 1 tells us would confirm what was happening on the Earth. For instance, just prior to the birth of Messiah, 2000-years ago, the Zodiacal Sign Scorpio (Oct. 22 – Nov. 21st) would also have included that of Libra, the Scales or Balance, symbolically fulfilling the weighing of the heart and subsequent destruction by the 'Swarms'- Arov - Ammit to follow, and a fact known in the Egyptian Book of the Dead.

For additional validation of our thesis, consider the value of the Hebrew word for Scorpions – Akrab, which is 372, the same as H#6212, עשב, `eseb, grass, which is interestingly, the Hebrew word for grass or green thing these beasts are told not to hurt – in the Plagues of the Greater Exodus found in Revelation 9:4. Moreover, the letters forming `eseb, can be rearranged to form שבע, sheva, 7, covenant, oath, to be filled, satisfied, to have an abundance! Satisfying our contention that these scourges are part of the Covenant oath of YHVH to judge the earth and its inhabitants because of sin!

Unbeknownst to most, the timing of these events of the plagues here in Exodus, coincided with a calendar change that would have made their occurrence the same months as that of Noah's flood, which began on the 17th day of the 2nd month.[#10] Based on Exodus 12 *"this shall be the beginning of months"* – Nissan instead of Tishri, the flood would have begun with the gates or fountains of the deep opening on Cheshvan 17. Each month would have been 30-days. By calculating each full moon of 2020 rather than the crescent, the 17th of Cheshvan is NOV. 3rd! Will the fountains open and unleash their swarms? I think the political events of last year (2020) became a smokescreen of sorts!

For instance, the 2020 presidential election was the greatest worldwide diversion in history! What happened while all eyes were on this event? Nov. 3rd 2020 = 11+3+40=54. 666666666. 54 is the gematria of H#3921, לכד, leked, to seize, capture, as in a trap or pit. From Nov. 3rd to April 1st = 150 days.

Curiously, the close of this aforementioned event takes place in the middle of Pesach: However, the full moon is March 28th which would technically be the beginning of the Feast of Unleavened Bread, the 15th of Nissan!

This mysterious circumstance is preceded by a rare "Blue Moon" on All Hallows' Eve (Halloween) occurring once every 18-19 years! 18 it the value of chatta, to sin or miss the mark, while 19 is the Value of Chavah! If you add the two together you get 37, the value of Balah, (Daniel 7:25) to wear out as in a MENTAL sense! This time, Chavah-Eve, the Bride of Messiah, will not fail as the Word has renewed Her Mind! Romans 12:1-3: The Spirit and The Bride say Come!

[#10] For additional calendar change information see my book: *Ezekiel's Wheel Within A Wheel*. http://www.ccbpublishing.com/dmathews.html

The 5th Plague - Exodus 9:1
The 5th Plague: A Grievous Murrain?[#11]

As we saw in the beginning of our exposition of Israel in Goshen, YHVH severed or made a distinction between the Lands of Israel and Egypt and their Peoples. Here now, we find the distinction increases to include a severing to include their cattle in the field:

Cattle here, is the Hebrew word, H#4735, מקנה, miqnah, that broadly describes all the 'herds' of both Nations; I.E. the horses, and asses, camels, oxen and sheep of each Nation. I propose that these events are both 'literal and parabolic' containing powerful, life-sustaining directions that are hidden until the proper season for those "to whom it is given to know"!

This 'cattle plague' seems to represent a Union of Houses, the "Lost Sheep and Judah". [*Some differ regarding banners*] A

[#11] Sabine Alex http://www.torah-illustrations.blogspot.com/
Used with permission.

Union for what purpose, against what foe you ask?

Toward that end, my curiosity was piqued by the specifics of these 'cattle', as their banners or ensigns that depicted ancient Tribal affiliation are shown in these plagues as well. For example here, we have Gad-horses, Ephraim-asses, Issachar-camel, Joseph-ox, and Judah-sheep/ram.

If anything, we've learned that Torah is layered with hidden information, secreted from the casual observer in the garments of such enigmatic parables. Consequently, in order to grasp what is really being shown here in this 5th plague, we must rummage deep into the hidden recesses and ask how will this affect the future Greater Exodus?

Beforehand, prior to the 5th plague YHVH warns Pharaoh: "אתה כי אם-מאן" Ki im-ma`en attah – If you refuse, this is what will happen. That phrase has a value of 568, the same as *Nephach Nephesh – To breathe away or give up the Soul*! Remember, this follows our previous explanation found in the Egyptian Book of The Dead wherein a soul whose heart is heavy is handed over to the Fallen Ones to devour!

This leads one to believe that by this time Pharaoh has given himself over wholly to the fallen angelic or demonic spirits motivating him to rebel against YHVH. As we fast forward, the patterns in the Exodus plagues divulge that, in like manner, they are identical to the plagues of Revelation, and as such, serve an ominous warning that the fate of many purported Believers may be sealed by this time!

This action, though ancient in scope, is reminiscent of the much more modern intent of today's DNA manipulation wherein the masses are inoculated with a cocktail of Pharmakeia, which is quite capable of disabling the God-Gene, thought to be hidden in the pineal gland of the forehead. These ingredients are going to be found in all of the WHO and UNITED NATIONS recommended immunizations that will be Militarily Enforced, including that of the coming C-19 vaccination we've warned of previously. (As of this writing it is mid-April 2021.

The KJV of Exodus 9:3 is rather innocuous in its translation here. However, the Hebrew gives a better understanding of the breadth of this horrific plague or pestilence which many believe is seen also in:

> Revelation 6:8 *And I looked, and behold a pale horse: and his name that sat on him was Death, and Hell followed with him. And power was given unto them over the fourth part of the earth, to kill with sword, and with hunger, and with death-plague, and with the beasts of the earth.*

The ominous words of the Prophet of Revelation portend a coming Plague whose scope is worldwide and of epic Biblical proportions. With this in the forefront of our minds, perhaps a look into the Hebraic descriptions is called for? Shall we?

- Grievous, H#3515　　כבד　　*Kaved*

    Pronounced kaved, and translated as heavy, oppressive.

- Murrain, H#1698　　דבר　　*Deber*

    Expressed as deber, a pestilence, a destroying word. The Greek Septuagint connects this word with that of Revelation 6:8 translated 'death' but more likely both were intended as pestilence. By way of reminder, the Book of Revelation is NOT in chronological order!

Is it possible then, in keeping with the "Sealing" of the Mind from our previous observations - that after the "Sealing" - YHVH is going to allow being released – a breath-a destroying deber-pestilence that becomes a Destroying Word judging the Kavod - heavy hearts of those weighed in the balance? How will one survive? Once again this should be familiar as the Ancient Egyptian Book of the Dead suggests as much!

Taking to account the seriousness of the above calamity, perhaps a reminder of the hope found in Psalms 91:3 is due? *Surely he shall* deliver *thee from the snare of the fowler, and from the noisome pestilence.*

This English word 'Noisome' derives from the Hebrew equivalent H#1942, הוה, havva, translated as desire, an engulfing ruin, yet comes from the root hava', indicating to blow as the wind or to breathe. This sounds like an air-borne scourge engulfing the Nations! The word for pestilence here is again – deber – a destroying word! It's worth noting, while we're at it, the etymology of the word for 'deliver', H#5337, rendered נצל: nasal, to deliver from another's hand. It can also indicate to draw off, to tear one away, or to snatch away. There's also a unique English word translated as nasal (Having to due with the nostrils, breath) and we note a subtle Edenic connection to the Hebrew word for 'deliver', H#5337, נצל: nasal!

It would seem the context here deals with the breath or word of YHVH delivering one from the air born, deber-pestilence - a destroying word of another or, allowing that pestilence to descend upon those whose hearts are weighed in the balance, and are hardened and judged!

**Remember YHVH's Word is LIGHT! It must be separated from darkness!

How Can We Know What to Expect?

Now, stop a second! We believe that Light is sound that was once light and is now slowed down. As such, perchance you'll remember how sound is 'heard'? The vibrations from wind, breath, etc. move across the eardrum, where these sounds – vibrations are collected, catalogued and translated into cogent thoughts in the MIND! Have you ever noticed that when one has a hearing debility, that the speech is also affected?

Therefore, if the MIND is sealed by the enemies' Electro-Magnetic frequencies and as a result, one cannot hear or receive the נשמת חיים, Nishmat Chayim – The Breath of Lives or Breaths of LIGHTS - we have no shielding mechanism for protecting ourselves! By the way, Nishmat can also be translated as 'the mind or intellect'.

Now you understand Philippians 2:5 *Let this mind be in you, which was also in Messiah Yahshua!* The Greek word for mind, phroneo, comes from phren (fra'n) indicating the diaphragm - breathing and phrasso, to fence in, block up, stop up! Technically, your ears, nose, mouth and MIND, along with the skin, are all intimately involved in ones' ability to breathe! Each of these areas is directly affected by the application of both Light and Sound! Observe: Mark 4:22,23: If I'm correct, it seems these Plagues are coded in parabolic or enigmatic language, intended to be understood by only those who 'rightly divide the Word of Truth!

> *For there is nothing hid, which shall not be manifested; neither was any thing kept secret, but that it should come abroad. If any men have ears to hear, let him hear.*

The text here plainly tells us that what is **hidden or cryptic will be made visible** if only one can hear??? Again, the link between hearing and sight is shown. Is this 5th plague about to reveal something that the Enemy's occult legions thought was hidden in plain sight? Yet, our protection or redemption available on the condition of - if only Man can hear!

For that reason, it is highly plausible that this Plague could actually be more than a physical disease or plague killing the cattle of Egypt!

**Remember even the Sages believe leprosy (A form of plague) came from Lashon ha'ra, 'the Evil tongue. Tongue, Lashon has the same value – 380 as Egypt, Mitsrayim! The number 380 is also the value of נשל, sounding the same as נצל – nasal above and meaning to draw away, pull off, to remove something! Is the cloaking garment or curtain about to be removed? Further, let me remind you it is assumed by most scholars that each plague represented a judgment against a god-idol of Egypt. We must assume the same here: But whose gods?

What if, for argument's sake, this plague is in response to the reinstitution of animal sacrifice and a 3rd-Temple worship (Quite possibly a mirror of Egypt's idolatry), after all, Pharaoh is literally translated "His Great House" and mirrored by the latter Greater House of the Greater Exodus which will be juxtaposed to the building of the HOUSE OF ISRAEL-YHVH!

What if, in competition with the True Temple of His Presence, and the Maqowm – The Place – That Altar of living sacrifice as detailed in Romans 12 - we find out almost too late and to the chagrin of many, that the enemy has knavishly co-mingled the DNA of those animals designated as 'sacrificial' (Having been affected by this cattle plague) with that of the Nephylim or Fallen Ones in order to have the Temple Mount Faithful blindly set up and make an offering formed from corrupt DNA, after his, The Beast's image in obeisance, albeit, ignorantly perhaps, to this monstrous – god of this world – chimera!

A purported 'holy offering' on what is surely going to be called the Altar of YHVH – therefore in response – YHVH Himself eliminates the seed of the Serpent/Nephylim! In passing here, the above Hebrew word for "The Place" is Maqowm and has a value of 186, the same as the phrase *"after his image"*.

**See Revelation 13:14 that speaks of making an image to this beast!

While contemplating this, I also found it disconcerting that the Hebrew word for leprosy, H#6879, צרע, tsara, meaning to strike down, a scourge, has the same Tzade-Resh root as Mitsrayim – Egypt. Further, that root stem indicates to burn, to be constricted, inflamed, a hoarseness, distress, to scream, and to roar. All of which are symptoms of viral infections associated with 'AIRBORN' weaponized - inhaled into the nasal passages, absorbed through the skin or eyes - viruses! This is too improbable to make up Reader!

If this is so, how apropos that the recent worldwide release of the Covid-19 pandemic, touted a universal scourge, is also said to have originated out of Chinese experimentation with gene editing and the hybridization of humans and animals! A horrific scenario, thus prompting immediately, the idea of wearing a Mask – to inhibit the SPEAKING OF TORAH and thus, to cover/hide HIS – YHVH's - IMAGE IN THE EARTH – ADAM! Without the speaking of His Word, which is the release of that healing light, the lack of which, results in darkness upon the land and a plague-like scripted game plan from the enemy!

Moreover, the English word 'mask'[#12] conveniently comes from the Hebrew word Masak meaning a curtain, veil, screen, etc. But, is also the root of masekah - an image, idol, and an alliance! Ignorance of the Law offers no excuse! Could compliance to forced mask wearing by a docile 'public' in effect, be a form of loyalty and devotion shown to the Beast and thus, mindlessly draw the world into an alliance with the IMAGE of the BEAST? Whose Image are we projecting? Oh, you don't think so????

The word "mask" appeared in English in the 1530s, from Middle an ancient French *masque* "covering to hide or guard the face",

---

[#12] https://en.wikipedia.org/wiki/Mask Public Domain.

derived in turn from the Italian Maschera, from Medieval Latin "masca" – mask, specter, and nightmare. This word is of uncertain origin, perhaps from Arabic maskharah "buffoon", from the verb sakhira "to ridicule". However, it may also come from Provencal mascarar "to black (the face)" or the related Catalan mascarar, Old French mascurer. This in turn is of uncertain origin – perhaps from a Germanic source akin to English "mesh", but perhaps from *mask-* "black", a borrowing from a pre Indo-European language. One German author claims the word "mask" is originally derived from the Spanish *más que la cara* (literally, "more than the face" or "added face"), which evolved to "máscara", while the Arabic "maskharat" – is referring to the buffoonery which is possible only by disguising the face – would be based on these Spanish roots. There are other related forms in Hebrew *masecha* = "mask"; the Arabic *maskhara* = "he ridiculed, he mocked", *masakha* = "he transformed"

If no Scourge is connected why does YHVH allow the Cattles' Destruction?

We must also recollect that all life is precious to YHVH and the arbitrary destruction of the entirety of Egypt's cattle, not to mention the peoples in both instances found in Exodus and here in Revelation was not the result of a Divine malevolence neither a frivolous whim! Please take note of Genesis 9: 12-17, wherein YHVH details the Covenant between Noah and all creatures upon the earth, whereat He promises to not ever again destroy them all! What is happening then?

Once more, let us call to mind the precedent set in the conquest of the Promised Land in which event all the men; women and cattle of the 7-Canaanite Nations were destroyed! So, what exactly is going on? Observe, the root stem of Canaan, H#3665, כנע, Cana, is etymologically related to Qanah or קין, Qayin-Cain. If we read Cana backwards: Ayin-Nun-Kaf, it gives us the cognate to Anak – Ayin-Nun-Qof – the infamous Mighty One, the name of which has a value of 220 the same as the word Nephylim! These Beings and their Cattle had comingled DNA!

Am I suggesting a relationship between this 5th plague, the Grievous Murrain that fell upon the Cattle of the World/Egypt and a future Greater Exodus plague that also falls, as a result of both nations intermingling their seed with that of the Nephylim – that GMO seed which is sown into their cattle? :(

Chapter 4

Where's the Proof?
Hidden Agendas Revealed

As we take a painstaking look back at the Hebrew word used as the object of the Grievous Murrain of chapter 4 i.e. 'cattle', H#4735, מקנה, pronounced 'miqnah' not much of a clue is found until we look at the first place it's used: Genesis 4:20 where it supposedly describes the vocation of Jabal, the 6th descendant in the lineage of Cain.

**Please Note: *And Adah bare Jabal: he was the father of such as dwell in tents, and of such as have cattle.*

There will be future descendants of JABAL who will resurrect this vocation: So the relations between Tent -Temple and such as have cattle must be explored!

This KJV casually remarks that Jabal was the father of those who dwelt in tents – AND – here is where the KJV gets weird...the Masorets translations supplied the italicized words and '*of such as have*' which is followed by the Hebrew word for cattle, miqnah. (Interestingly, there are 32 letters in this verse here, giving us the numeric value of the Hebrew word H#3582, כחד, kachad, meaning to hide, conceal, to cut off, be destroyed as in Exodus 9:15 where Pharaoh and his people are 'cut off – kachad'.)

**Pay close attention.

If we parse this verse properly, the word translated as a noun – miqnah/cattle - could also be written in the Hebrew grammatical hiphil stem expressing a verbal action! In this case the Mem prefix is a causative action – causing, provoking – it is the origin of, source of the root: קנה, Qanah – to get, acquire, to provoke to jealousy! Wait aren't we speaking of cattle Mi-qanah? Perhaps something else entirely is hidden in the depths of the Hebrew language.

For the moment, doesn't it seem odd that so many connections to hiding, concealing, and secrets, or that something puzzling or cryptic is being highlighted by these links? Am I out of my mind conversely, to propose that Jabal dwelt – yashab, H#3427, ישב, to inhabit, to dwell with, or cohabitate as in marriage – rather, *in a Tent of sorts that provoked YHVH to jealousy* instead of merely being the progenitor of shepherds?

The idea of this word yashab pictures a home, a dwelling where Husband and Wife produce seed. Further, if we look at the Hebrew word pictures then simply rearrange the same letters, they would style יבש, and would give us the Hebrew word yabbash, hinting at something that is dry, barren, and is related to buwsh – shame! You must bear in mind that the ancient picture of The Tent symbolizes the intimate chamber where the Seed is released.

Picture this: The Seed of Adam has been cut off (Abel) – while Cain has been banished into the land of Nod, a.k.a. the Tohu V'Bohu wasted and barren place. Could Jabal be thus establishing a fertility clinic mixing the genes of the Fallen Ones with his own and that of his cattle? Remember the same pattern with Abram and Sarai: Pharaoh attempts to insert his seed into her barren womb! In response, YHVH inserts the Hebrew letter "HEY" into their names: Hey has a gematria of 5, the same as the word Alef-Dalet – Ad, the fire vapor or mist upon the earth watering the Garden!

In passing, both the Hebrew words yashab and yabbash have a gematria of 312, the same as בני מרי, B'nei Mari – Perverse Children and החרטמים, h'chartumiym, The Magicians, those who displayed supernatural powers on behalf of Pharaoh/Egypt and on behalf of the coming Anti-Messiah who will display lying signs and wonders! Your mind is your womb! It is going to be sealed – either by YHVH or Satan!

To add to the parabolic twist here, the Septuagint has the word SKEIN for Tent, from which we get the English 'SKIN'. Did Jabal have a mixed DNA skin garment consisting of a unique type of skin, skein, a Tent or Tabernacle from Cain's lineage, which he continued and wherein he, like Cain, produced offspring who provoked YHVH to jealousy? If this is too outrageous, remember the Wilderness Tabernacle, designed in the form of the Man, also had a skin/skein garment covering it!

In addition, as we look deeper at the Genesis 4 account of Jabal, the 6th generation from Cain, we find he has two brothers whose names have that same 3-letter root, Yod-Bet-Lamed - יבל, Jabal - Yabal – Jubal and Tubal Cain: This root forms the Hebrew word Yovel – indicating a release, a setting free, an overturning of slavery. In its purest form it indicates to transport, or transfer something from one place to another! Could it be this Jabal watched over a Tent or Portal, a gateway of sorts allowing the introduction or transportation of the Watchers/Fallen Ones into the world? If so, is it possible the initiation of the coming 3rd Temple and its perverted Sacrifices (The Grievous Murrain) also forms a portal or transport for the introduction of the King of the Pit?

Each of these men Jabal, Jubal and Tubal Cain are 6th generation – from Cain – 6+6+6? Incidentally, Cain, H#7014, קין, originates from the same root as this word for cattle – Miqnah – The Mem indicates the source, origin of Qanah – jealousy! Additionally,

666 is the value of סתור, satuwr, meaning to hide or conceal, preventing someone from knowing: Could there be a connection to hiding the Image of Jealousy?

Satuwr is also cognate with Satar, a skin eruption, boils, tumors, etc. Perhaps, YHVH is giving all who participate in the False Messiah's Temple a warning of eternal repercussions? – This Temple is itself, an "Image" H#6755, צלם, Tselem, the word used in Daniel 2:31 to describe Nebuchadnezzar's statute depicting the End-Time conglomerate Kingdom! Moreover, Tselem has a value of 160, the same as Naphal – the root of Nephylim!

FYI, the Sages depict Esau as having killed Nimrod, who was supposedly wearing the 'SKIN' Garment of Cain/Jabal: Esau is depicted as a Satyr – related to the above Satuwr – a man hybrid he-goat of demonic proportions. It is my position that Esau has currently turned the tables on Jacob and is now masquerading – disguised as – JACOB! You will not be seeing Esau in his Chimera-garment, only his Jacobean Image - until he believes he has taken back the final piece of his Right of First Born – the Priesthood, at which time he will be seen worldwide for who he really is!

For centuries, the Jacobean Families have controlled the Crown! The 2020 Corona-Crown virus is one of their breathed out children!

Let's Continue to Look at Miqnah-Qanah-Cattle

Genesis 4:1 reveals Eve-Chavah birthing Cain-קין, Qayin, and declaring "I have gotten, H#7069, קנה, Qanah, to possess, acquire, to provoke to jealousy - a man from YHVH". Why not translate consistently and say I have gotten cattle from YHVH? What indeed, could have been the source of Eve's provocation, if not the comingling of the serpent's seed with that of Man?

That being said, did the Miqnah – Cattle of Egypt and those of the Revelation Cattle have mixed DNA of sorts, which in someway, perhaps if ingested could affect the human genome, the resulting hybridization provoking YHVH to a jealous wrath?

Likewise, could this JABAL - 6th generation reveal a sci-fi like, 6-G technology - far surpassing that of the heinous 5-G, thus, becoming a tool for the mingling of the DNA of Man with that of the Fallen Ones? Nebuchadnezzar saw this day in his vision in Daniel 2:41-43 of the statue representing the 'kingdoms' whose feet are mingled: Iron with miry clay.

Note verse 43: *And whereas thou sawest iron mixed with miry clay,* **they shall mingle themselves with the seed of men*: but they shall not cleave one to another, even as iron is not mixed with clay.*

Furthermore, the root Beit-Lamed in Jabal connotes a mixing of sorts. It is related to Babel – confusion by mixing and if we add the Tav prefix it forms H#8397, תבל, tebel, translated as perversion, incest. It is a strong word condemning human-animal copulation as well! It can't happen you say! Yet, the soon to be mandatory Covid-19 vaccination and the Avian Bird flu behind it, will undoubtedly contain a unique strain of DNA altering (NOTE THAT WORD ALTER-ALTAR) materials that will bring you to the Altered -Altar of those who are preparing the Tent of Jealousy – Miqnah! The Tent of Jabal!

Each of these 'vaccines' have a Genetically Modified Light/Word/Seed/Breath in them called: Luciferase - Luciferase combines an enzymatic substrate from a substance called luciferin along with oxygen and ATP, which leads to a release of light energy somewhat like the phosphorescent glow of seawater and fireflies. Using the vitality release by these enzymes scientists were able to produce a similar reaction that could oversee certain biological procedures such as gene locution, bimolecular binding and cell longevity each of which helped to take advantage of the Luciferase's powerful energy. These terms indicate the presence of gene altering capabilities that are intrinsic to these vaccines!

The apocalyptic Pale Horse Rider of Revelation 6:8 brings to mind this plague! Pale is <u>Gk. #5515</u>, chloros, a yellow-green color! The Greek word for horse, <u>G#2462</u>, hippos, is remarkably similar to the Hippocratic oath taken by all physicians! This compound word comes from: hippo-horse and crates-ruler, horse ruler! A derivative 'hypocritos' refers to actors who wore masks during plays at the theater. A hypocrite is one who shows one face to the world while hiding another underneath! Are you so naïve that you cannot see the inevitable connections? Dear Reader! It is time to awaken from your slumber!

Now let's look a bit further! This adds a bit more curiosity to Revelation 18:4 "come out of her – Jabal-Babel – the Tent of Miqnah – Jealousy"! Else you partake of her plagues!

**Note the Greek word for 'her'; <u>G#846</u>, autos, translated as a feminine pronoun it derives from aer, a-a'r, a baffling wind or breath!

Again, Jabal dwelt in a tent, <u>H#168</u>, אהל, 'ohel, rendered 'tent'. Its gematria – 36, (6x6) is also that of Eleh, to swear an oath, to curse, and to covenant. It indicates a terebinth or long-lived tree planted in confirmation of an oath, it also hints at an idol. Further it is the value of the Hebrew word badal, meaning to divide or separate.

Though innocuously translated as 'tent', its broader meaning hints at a gathering place (Tent-Tabernacle-Temple) perhaps where a Tower of Babel incident could occur! The Tower of Babel and all such of its kind were the formation of a deliberate and mock societal gathering for the express purpose of interchanging thoughts, language and other cultural expressions. In such groups, minds could be sharpened and thus amalgamate into large collaborative efforts such as a universal exchangeable language! This is the plan of the Global Elite as of this writing!

Is it possible that Jabal dwelt in a Tent –Tabernacle -Temple construct where those gathered somehow provoked YHVH to jealousy, which jealousy is somehow linked not only to modifying the DNA of animals - a genetically modified chimera-hybrid of sorts - designated for sacrifice, but also for the control (Mixing/Babel) of the language of creation the Hebrew Tongue and the language of Torah and as such, indirectly responsible for hiding the 'true' location of the House of YHVH? It's interesting to compare our narrative to the gospel accounts of Yahshua's cleansing the Temple of those whom He called 'thieves' who were selling animals for sacrifice. He forces an embargo on such in Mark 11:15-18. Most scholars believe this occurred at Pesach or Passover and thus to have been the catalyst for His death! Food for thought here: If a world-wide plague affecting all of Egypt's – the World's cattle ensues, where will the 3rd-Temple animal sacrifices come from if not these hybridized creations? Just saying...

As we continue, the gematria of Jabal, Jubal and Tubal-Cain equals 528, the same hertz frequency of the ancient Solfeggio note 'MI' – the musical note associated with that of DNA repair (or corruption if usurped) and miracles. Could these men have been complicit with the Nephylim or Fallen Ones in crossing over the boundaries established by YHVH for procreation of both Man and Animals? Not sure if such is possible, then please look at the following. In 2010, there was a disaster at an oilrig owned by BP called the Deepwater Horizon, causing it to leak millions of barrels worth of oil into the Gulf of Mexico.

An electromagnetic energy expert, John Hutchison of Vancouver, along with his wife and research partner, Nancy Lazaryan Hutchison, decided to do something to help. They placed a device that emits frequencies on the beach, about 25 feet from the water, and used 528 Hz and other Solfeggio frequencies to treat the water. They only did this for four hours, but the waters had miraculously cleared by the next morning. In fact, the water had so improved that dolphins, fish, and crabs returned to the area, when just a day before those same waters would have been lethal for marine life.[#13]

With the above in mind, it would seem that at the very least a connection to the last Goshen, albeit a spiritual or soul's link can be found in our hypothesis that a divine Holy of Holies relationship is revealed in the Place of Marking – The Forehead – which includes The Nasal, Hearing, and Mind aspect of a man. Again, the Sages believe the sense of smell (connected by its Edenic roots to nasal) was the only one of the Man's senses not corrupted by the Fall!

Incidentally, the Edenic origins of "Nasal" add intrigue as there is a definite connection between hearing and breathing where the middle ear is an extension of the respiratory air spaces of the nose and the sinuses and is lined with a respiratory membrane. Thus, breathing and hearing and the above word for deliver - 'nasal' are etymologically related! How convenient that Covid-19 testing involves the raping of the Nasal passage by a phallic swab containing the very pathogenic virus or SEED – masked innocently in the caring hands of the Agents of Agenda 21.

For your reference, 21 is the Value of the Hebrew word H#2327, חובה, chowbah, the name of the Place (Genesis 14:15) where Abraham destroyed (The Slaughter of the Kings – Corona) those who took his Nephew Lot prisoner! The Hebrew name Lot means garment. Chowbah means hiding place! The city was physically situated on the 'left hand' – Semowl – an outer garment hiding something within – of Damascus! Damascus is an intriguing word being a compound of; Dam, meaning blood, while Masaq - Mem-Shin-Qof indicates the heir or steward who

---

[#13] https://www.opednews.com/articles/Miracle-in-the-Gulf-of-Mex-by-Heather-Dodge-101212-589.html Used with permission, per Heather Dodge.

has the legal right to inherit! Masaq is related to Masak – Mask, to hide or cover!

The Seed of Abraham will inherit the Earth and will be protected in Goshen while the Greater Exodus Plagues expose the identity of the Hidden Ones and their Agenda!

Exodus 9:8-17
The 6th Plague: Boils with Blains[#14]

Before we take an in-depth look at *'Boils with Blains'*, it would help to understand the circumstances that lead to this 6th plague. Primarily, there's a subtle transition-taking place in this text with this 6th plague. In our introduction we saw Aaron the High Priest initiate the first 3: The 4th and 5th are ascribed to YHVH and

---

[#14] Sabine Alex http://www.torah-illustrations.blogspot.com/
Used with permission.

now, this 6th plague to Moshe. We've shown that these understated references are actually ingenious ways developed to hide clues that will reveal a future Greater Exodus connection.

For instance: Moshe clearly acts on behalf of YHVH, in effect, being a "Messiah-Figure" in His stead. Thus, the role of Aaron is that of one who is cast as the personal spokesman I.E. the Prophet of Moshe!

To find their alter ego (Note alter/altar this contrast will become apparent as we continue) or false counterpart in End-Times eschatology we need only look at Revelation 13 where we see two distinct Beings operating from 2-different levels of authority.

#1 The Beast out of the Sea and #2 The Beast out of the Earth. One is clearly the Anti-Messiah the other commonly referred to as "The False Prophet". They will stand in stark opposition to the Messiah and His Prophet!

It is my opinion that the Mantle of Elijah rests upon a Remnant of the Outcasts who will collectively stand in the latter role of True Prophets of YHVH and will attend the TRUE ALTAR AND TRUE TEMPLE OF YHVH - This gives us the Moshe-Aaron effect!

Heavenly Witness - The Grand Conjunction:

As a Heavenly Witness to the above premise, on 12/21/20 we saw what is termed 'a Grand Conjunction' between the two 'KING' planets – Jupiter and Saturn! They have not been this close (0.1 degrees) since July 16, 1623. Further, this event occurs in the Constellation Aquarius – the dawning of which – is upon us! Many are calling this the Great Transformation! FYI the Strong's number H#1623 gives us גרד, garad, a piece of pottery used to scrape Job's body after being stricken with BOILS, once again linking us to this 6th plague! Coincidence?

Ironically, it is highly possible that Yahshua was born at a previous conjunction of these two in the constellation Pisces on 7/15/7-BC. This set the cycle for the transformation in the procession of the Zodiacal Houses and announced the birth of Messiah! I believe this conjunction will see the revealing of the 1st Beast in a Religious/Political birthing!

Though a Gregorian calendar date is used, the numbers of that event were intriguing. 12+21+20=53, the gematria of נבא, nava, to prophecy!

Additional confirmation can be found in the precession of the Poles. At present, the Pole star Drago (who entwines 1/3 of the stars) is being replaced, perhaps cast down – as shown in Revelation 12:7-13 - whose place is not found anymore - by Polaris.

This is a Stellar Prophecy of the contrast between the Fallen Morning Star – Lucifer – a.k.a. Saturn and the Risen Morning Star – Yahshua – Jupiter the Planet known as Zadek, צדק! Like Draco, Lucifer only partially controlled 9 of the Priestly breastplate stones - while this transition will see the restoration of the true King and Priest contrasted against the Counterfeit! Thus, restoring the full 12-Breastplate stones of the High Priest after the Order of Melchizedec!

As a further confirmation to the power of this season the ancient Mayans believed 12-21-20 to be the end of the AGE! It is my opinion the Beast/Dragon was in effect, cast down at this season, and the Abyss opened! In contrast, for those SEALED by YHVH a simultaneous release of power, will result in an upload of knowledge and wisdom necessary for the implementation and demonstration of HIS Kingdom!

Those who are sealed by the enemy will receive strong delusion causing them to believe a lie. Delusion comes from the Greek 'plan-ay', a wandering or straying about. Does the Land of Nod, alias 'to wander' as in Cain's habitation, sound familiar?

**Note 2Thessalonians 2:12. *That they all might be damned who believed not the truth, but had pleasure in unrighteousness.* What is coming cannot be rebuked! YHVH has set this into motion!

The Beast Comes

The Septuagint describes this 1st Being out of the Sea, as a Beast, Gk. #2342, tha-re'-on, from tha'ra, a trap or trapper/hunter of men who rises up from the Sea. The English word *Rises* is translated from the Gk. #305 a-na-bi-'no - a compound of the preposition *Ana* – from, among, through, out of and *ba'-ses*, the foot! Will this Beast rise out of, the feet?

We'll examine the Vision of Nebuchadnezzar in a moment. First, note what Jeremiah says regarding the hunters who are coming during what most consider the Great Tribulation!

**Note:

> Jeremiah 16:16 *Behold, I will send for many fishers, saith YHVH, and they shall fish them: and after will I send for many hunters, and they shall hunt them from every mountain, and from every hill, and out of the holes of the rocks.*
>
> Jeremiah 16:19 *Oh YHVH, my strength, and my fortress, and my refuge in the day of afflictions — the Gentiles shall come unto thee from the ends of the earth, and shall say, Surely our fathers have inherited lies, vanity, and things wherein there is no profit.*

The English word 'Vexer' translated afflictions above is from H#6869, צרה, tsarah, as in trouble (Jacob's) tribulation, a Vexer

The Exodus Keys

rival wife – Babylon the Harlot is that Vexer and we must remove ourselves from her.

As I mentioned a moment ago, this 1st – Beast will arise out of the feet, a reminder of the dreadful prophetic interpretation by Daniel, of Nebuchadnezzar's vision of the latter day kingdom whose feet - *ba'-ses* - were of iron and miry clay! The Kingdom associated with this Beast comprises the feet and toes. Please note the Hebrew words for these two English nouns.

- Feet, H#7271   רגל   *Regel*

   Translated feet, it is also a euphemism for the male pudenda or privates. It comes from the root ragal, to spy out, slander, a talebearer. To tread upon washed garments. Regel has a value of 233, the same as Bechorah – 1st Born, birthright. This Beast will come exercising the BERTH RIGHT GIVEN TO HIM BY OUR FATHERS AND FORFEITED BY OUR ACQUIESENCE! If you don't understand what I just said, spend a few moments on the Internet searching the origin of the Birth Certificate!

- Toes, H#677   אצבע   *Eetsbah*

   It is rendered 'toes', yet originates from an obscure root, tseba, indicating a versicolored or divers colored garment. Is it just I or does this seem an attempt at counterfeiting or slandering the lineage-DNA of the 10-toes-Tribes by inserting corrupt seed into those that have been scattered into the earth?

Furthermore, Etsbah has a value of 163, the same as zenuniym, from Zonah, an infamous Hebrew word indicating fornication, adultery, but also - FOREIGN COMMERCE – as in SEA MERCHANTS! From the day of your birth/berth you have been bought and sold, traded upon the Securities and Exchange Commission by the Elite! The Enemy is coming to Collect His! If you plan on exiting Babylon as commanded in Revelation 18:4, then you'd be well served to learn the truths being shared here. This Beast, like the ancient Mighty Hunter known as Nimrod of Babylon, is in reality according to the Hebrew language himself a Nephylim, or hunter who preys on or Consumes men! Ironically, the English word cannibalism – gets its origin from the compound of Cain and Ba'al – Cainba'al - the original MANEATER – and this hideous practice is on the increase worldwide!

Allow me to clarify. It is without rebuttal, that the current Covid-19 vaccine, and many others have aborted fetal tissue as part of their ingredients. The word for 'eat' in Hebrew is akal – to eat, or consume. If one takes any of these diabolical cocktails of what I call a witch's brew, one has consumed the fetus! Abhorrent as it seems most simply comply having long since lost awareness of the God Gene that is the moral compass of Man!

We can add emphasis here once again, by looking back at Nimrod. It is fitting to note that the original inception of ancient Babylon, the Kingdom associated with both beasts above, began with this Nimrod (Genesis 10:8,9) who himself was referred to as: *"A mighty hunter before YHVH..."* KJV. The word for hunter here is H#6718, ציד, tsayid, and derives from the root meaning: to lie in wait for, to capture, or to lay snares. He was in fact, a 'hunter of men'. *Remember Jeremiah 16: 16 above?

Nimrod by David Scott, circa 1832[#15]

The previous verse indicates that he '*began to be a mighty one in the earth*'. Began is the Hebrew word H#2490, חלל, chalal, to profane, defile, to prostitute, eat, inheritance and to sexually defile. The Chet-Lamed root hints at twirling, a twisting: While mighty one is translated from H#1368, גבור, gibbowr, mighty, giant, etc.

From the forensic evidence in the Hebrew language, it seems Nimrod participated in gene manipulation with the Giant Ones! As some of you may know, archeologists claim to have found

---

[#15] https://en.wikipedia.org/wiki/Nimrod#/media/File:Nimrod_(painting).jpg Public Domain.

Nimrod's tomb and efforts underway to clone him. He was said to be 1/3 man and 2/3rds god – 66.6 percent: It is highly possible that the Anti-Messiah could have the cloned DNA of this Mighty One!

Moreover, this future Beast of Revelation will also be a Nephylim. Could both beasts be guilty of hunting men in order to use their DNA as an adjunct mingled with their own DNA in order to achieve immortality? *I will never give them my DNA you say?* Your parents did when your footprints – the Kaf – or title deed – were put in fresh ink on their Berth Bond Paper! The birth certificate! *Who wants their DNA tested, surely we want to find our ancestors?* [Sarcasm mine] For a case in point see the following...

Does the Word Adrenochrome Sound Familiar?

Adrenochrome is a chemical compound with the molecular formula $C_9H_9NO_3$ produced by the oxidation of adrenaline. Adrenaline is a hormone, neurotransmitter, and medication. Adrenochrome is harvested from the adrenal/pituitary glands of a live victim! It is no accident that Wuhan, China the site of the Cov19 virus - the place where genetic animal/human hybrids were a constant experiment - was also a commercially available source of Adrenochrome for years! I'll leave it to you to connect the dots!

My curiosity was piqued by the molecular symbol above. Incredulous as it may seem, you may think surely the ELITE would never demonstrate their Magic or Witchcraft by hiding the following? 12/21/20 the Vaccine will probably be released! [I made this statement several months in these notes prior to release that did take place in mid-December] Now, let's look at that molecular formula $C_9H_9NO_3$:

First, the numbers 9+9+3 give us the value (21) of H# 2327,

The Exodus Keys

חובה, Chowbah, the city near Damascus where Abraham pursued and destroyed the Nephylim Kings. Genesis 14. Chowbah as we saw in our last segment means 'hiding place'. *Ironically, Saul/Paul was also on this same road to Damascus,* which we will connect later for another bizarre reality check!

Moreover, 21 is also the value of the Hebrew word H#2374, חזו, chezu, defined as a vision, a revelation. It is related to oracle. The sealing of the Forehead opens the 3RD EYE IN THE PITUITARY PINEAL GLAND ALLOWING THE WHOLE WORLD TO SEE to have vision, to prepare for the Oracle!

Further, the ordinal value of the C-H-N-O equals 40, the gematria of habal, חבל, to take a pledge to destroy. If you change the vowel points to hobel, it indicates a seaman who transports wares. The importance of this link cannot be overstated because the 1st Beast will arise out of the Sea! It is again, not coincidental that all commerce is regulated by Maritime Law – Law of the SEA!

Edenically, the Hebraic etymology of the letters and their English counterparts, relate to C-Gimmel, H-Hey, N-Nun, and the O vowel from -Vav. These letters phonetically sound remarkably like Gehenna, the place of the Dead, a.k.a. The Valley of Hinnom – *The cursed place where Israel offered their children in the Fire!* Gehenna was said to have 3-gates leading to the underworld: **1 in the Sea,** 1 in the wilderness-**Land**, 1 in Jerusalem! Will these Beasts of Revelation rise up in a final quest to 'resurrect' the DNA of the Fallen Ones in their attempt at world conquest? Already a specialized term for DNA gene splicing called CRISPR Cas9 has been in use for some time and is touted for use in a vaccine for COVID-19.

Lastly, regarding this point if you simply look at the English letters C-H-N-O you have the root of Cohen-The Levitical High Priestly lineage that I believe the 1st Beast will lay claim to, in support of his acceptance as false (Anti Messiah)! You also have the root of CHINA!

History reveals that ESAU (Masquerading as Jacob during the time of Yahshua) controlled this priesthood: The Romans sold the office to Anias and Caiaphas! ESAU is returning to collect his BERTH RIGHTS FROM THOSE IN COMMERCE, IN THE SEA WITH HIM! The UNIFORM COMMERCIAL CODE RULES THE SEA WORLD! Now you know why Disney movies and theme parks are introducing the innocent children to the SEA WORLD!

It seems most of Disney's theme parks and attractions, their rides and restaurants all play a role in the global enigmatic and hidden fraternity known as: The **S**ecret **S**ociety of **E**xplorers and **A**dventurers: SEA! Though what I'm writing may seem conspiratorial, it is, nonetheless, truth and has a biblical foundation, which has been maniacally twisted to suit their agendas like most of the 'magical' slight-of-hand techniques used by the Elite.

The Biblical precedent was set in motion when Jacob had his family to 'cross the SEA' in the form of the river Jabbok, H#2999, יבק, Yabboke, has a value of 113, the same as the Hebrew word Chukkah, which means a statute, law or custom, to engrave, or to cut into:

The root of Jabbok means an emptying, to make void, to fail or lay waste, to depopulate! The hidden repercussions of which had a far reaching effect upon the myriads of generations that today are suffering simply because Jacob forces his entire house to bow before Esau, with the exception of Benjamin – The Son of the Right Hand! As a result, it is Esau who today masquerades as Jacob and who has further exploited the birthright of all those Sons of Jacob scattered into the Nations! But, take heart dear Reader – that is soon to change!

I know that some may find fault with what I just said. However, one would do well to hear the matter before making a judgment. Please look at the following couple of paragraphs and then decide if you believe Jacob did the right thing.

Genesis 33:3 provides the scriptural backdrop here with what is described as the act of Jacob bowing 7-times. It is well documented that such bowing was the customary action of a Vassal before his overlord! According to Ancient Near East treaties this was an act of reverence whose origin was found in the Royal Courts! Take note of this verse number: 33:3 – I believe the English KJV – and their Masonic translators intentionally did this! 33rd degree Master Mason Illuminated! These are your overlords! To whom do you prostrate yourself?

In continuation, the expression *"seven and seven times I fall at the feet of the king, my lord"* is found more than fifty times in the Amarna letters.

This was an ironic and contrasting reversal of his (Jacob's) previous blessing in:

> Genesis 27:29 *Let peoples serve you, and nations bow down to you. Be lord over your brothers, and may your mother's sons bow down to you.*

Incredibly, many believe a connection exists between the Catholic Pope and the future Esau-Nimrod or Anti-Messiah figure and seeing as how the government of the Papacy is called the HOLY SEE-SEA he could function as Pope/High Priest and Imam uniting the 3-Crowns of those 'Heads'!

Before we return back to our detective work regarding the 2 Beasts of Revelation I want to spend a few moments expounding on the last paragraph and help to put into context the connection between the future Esau-Nimrod and the coming-Anti Messiah figure and how the foundation for his world-wide Kingdom was established in the pattern seen above.

Chapter 5

The Nimrod-Cain-Esau Connection

In retrospect, another interesting link can be found with Nimrod's relationship with Cain's lineage, where many Talmudic scholars believe the sister of Tubal-Cain, called Naamah (Genesis 4:22) later becomes the wife of Noah and betrays Noah by getting him drunk (Genesis 9) with wine like her latter-day counterpart, the Whore of Babylon who offers the world a cup of wine!

Though her Hebraic name Naamah, נעמה, H#5279, is translated as 'pleasant' the Nun-Mem root hints at despised, that which is vile. Further, the value of her name equals 165, the same as נפלה, nafalah, to fall or be cast down, the root of Nephylim, the ancient god-men or Mighty Ones. It is these fallen Beings and their return that I believe are being referenced by the well-known phrase of Matthew 24:37 associated with the 'End of Days' *[As it was in the days of Noah* – eating, drinking, giving in marriage.]

**See also Jeremiah 51:7, Revelation 16:19 regarding this day, in which Jeremiah declares Babylon will offer her wine to the Nations and as a result: ...*The Nations are mad (insane)*, H#1984, הלל, halal, the Hebrew has: יתהללו, yitholelu, (imperfect tense 3rd-person masc.) This could read: The Nations shall be (his) Halal's – this same noun used here is also seen as part of

Lucifer's name in Isaiah 14. Hallel ben Shachar!

The word for drunk (Genesis 9) above is: H#7937, שׁכר, shakar and is etymologically related to H#7837, שׁחר, shakhar, one who rises early, the morning, to seek early, to break or pry into something: As I said above, this is the 2nd part of the description of Lucifer's name found in Isaiah 14:12. Please take time to read the Hebrew text here and you'll find evidence proving that Lucifer attempted to break into the genetic code of the DNA of YHVH! The result is that the hybridized Luciferin DNA drives the Nations mad-insane! By now, you should be familiar with Proverbs 25:2 and hopefully, you will use it as a motivation to dig below the surface of the plain text. *It is the glory of God to conceal a thing: but the honour of kings is to search out a matter.*

As an example; Lucifer declares: "I will sit also upon the mount of the congregation: ואשב בהר-מועד – V'ashav b'har-mo'ed: Yashav implies the consummation of a marriage, But, note its etymological relationship with ESAU, עשו, (The letters Ayin and Alef are interchangeable) though Esau is translated 'hairy' its root means to make something happen. Lucifer planned to ESAU the Nations!

Further, the phrase b'har, in the mount, could read: Bet – in the house or bride, Har also indicates to impregnate. Next is Mo`ed, an appointed time, place, season, especially the Tent of Meeting. Lucifer has declared he will impregnate the bride in her house at an appointed time!

This precedent can be found again, if we follow the Hebrew of Genesis 9 and the episode with Noah and Ham, where we see his name - Ham, in Hebrew comes from the same root Chet-Mem – Cham, as the father (His name was Chamowr) of Shechem, it is this son who rapes Jacob's daughter Dinah! You'll see this connection later…hold these thoughts and…

David Mathews

Let's Return Back to Our Look at The Beast

Moving forward, this 1st Beast rises out of the Sea. Which is truly interesting as the Ancients believed there were 2 primordial Beasts; one which came from the abyss or oceanic (Sea) depths and referred to as Leviathan, the other which roamed the dry land or earth called Behemoth.

The KJV 'SEA' is both literal and euphemistic. Sea in ancient lore is the place of the dead and it's no coincidence the maritime phrase 'lost at sea' a term used for those considered dead. Ironically, in the occult maritime/sea world contrived by the Elites, a birth/berth certificate announces a shipping cargo being delivered by-to the DOCKtor. This certificate is a banking instrument and creates a fictional, non-living entity that will upon presentation, masquerade as the Living Man who is considered 'lost at sea'.

Moreover, the term "Sea" serves euphemistically as a reference for People in general. When we see the SEA giving up its dead, it can be taken both as the final resurrection of those departed Souls, as well as, a group who were thought to be dead – yet who will arise from the Sea-multitudes to rightfully assert their place as Ivrit – Hebrews, those who stand in opposition to this future Nimrod!

The above diatribe may seem a bit out of place, but please note the phrase - 'banking instrument'! Now, let's look at this Sea Monster: Leviathan.

- Leviathan, H#3882   לויתן

    It is rendered as 'dragon, sea monster'. Dragon is quite apropos considering our topic, as it represents the constellation of the Dragon and is a symbol of Babylon. Leviathan is from the root lava; to borrow, lend, a lender, to cause to borrow (Banking instruments?) to join, to intertwine, uniting with. Curiously, it is from the same root as Levi – to join to – the family 'Tribe' of both Aaron and Moshe!

The Tav-Nun suffix forms a root in words that mean 'taniyn – sea monster', tanna – a teacher, to repeat, set conditions, stipulate, to cause to bear fruit, to hire. It very well may be possible this Beast/Monster from the Sea is going to set conditions and stipulations in union with the Papacy, the House of Levi and the Christian Church and other pseudo religious organizations. Incidentally, the gematria of Leviathan – 496 - is the same as Malchut – Kingdom!

Many believe the connection to the Abyss and the paths through the Sea that serve, as portals to our world will open in the near future, allowing entrance to this Hybrid Super-hero 'MAN' who will be a clone of a charismatic world leader who seemingly 'dies' and is miraculously resurrected! This could be a literal death or a political-religious-public restoration of a ruined career or loss of power and authority! He is the epitome of Nebuchadnezzar's vision of the 10-iron toes spoken of by Daniel and referred to as 'iron mixed with miry clay'!

It is my opinion that he will usurp through the international cabal Banking/Financial System the role of 'Levitical High Priest' and the Papacy controlling the 'Crown of England' among others and set himself up as the object of worship.

Now, What About This 2nd Beast?

This 2nd Beast will perform miracles and force the Masses into blind worship of the 1st Beast. He arises out of the Land. In other words, out of those who have been "SALVAGED" from the SEA, and are now 'On The Land'; veiled perhaps as a contemporary "Christianized" Prophet/PROFIT, who has been established on the Land and is expecting their inheritance! The Greek calls him Behemoth.

- Behemoth, H#930   בהמות

    Translated as beast, probably an ancient hippopotamus like dinosaur. This 2nd Beast arises out of the earth. Daniel calls this earth - 'Miry Clay', H#2917, miry - טין, tiyn and clay, H#2635, חסף, chacaph. Tiyn comes from a root indicating damp dirt, but also something to be swept away. Chacaph is rendered clay, earthenware, but corresponds to 'scales', to peel away. Blindness in part will fall upon those who align themselves with this Beast and his system. This is part of the GREAT FALLING AWAY! 2Thessalonians 2:1-12!

Note the cognate Tet-Nun and Tav-Nun roots hinting that this Beast will also teach, set conditions, hire, and stipulate circumstances that will cause scales upon the Eyes of many who look upon the Image of the Beast! In particular, those blinded by religious traditions, which have been diabolically calculated to influence the decisions of many!

**Remember both Lenin and Karl Marx's infamous statement: *Religion is the opium of the People.*

This same concept of scales being upon the eyes of many is seen in Acts 9:18 where Saul a.k.a. Shaul, a devout, religious, Jewish, Levitical Zealot, who later becomes the Apostle Paul, is 1st seen as a *'type of Anti-Christ'* - further, this persecutor of Messiah was struck blind with a type of scales, from the Greek. #3013, lepis, to peel off as in a flake.

Paul is traveling on the road to Damascus, H#1834, דמשק, a compound word stemming from Dam-blood and Mesek – which means 'the heir apparent' – Paul thinking he is doing the right thing, as many do today, is found persecuting the followers of Yahshua (Jesus) fervently demonstrating his religious zeal in protecting the HIGH PRIEST of the Levitical system who he deems BLOOD HEIR APPARENT merely to be confronted by the ONLY GENUINE BLOOD - HEIR APPARENT – to the office of THE HIGH PRIEST – AFTER THE ORDER OF MELCHIZEDEK – none other than YAHSHUA, the Messiah!

It will benefit us immensely to make the connection here to the city of Damascus as well, because this ancient city will figure very prominently in the End-Days.

**Note the following:

Damascus is a central figure throughout Torah and lies in close proximity to the ancient lands *occupied to this day* – by the Nephylim! This pulls back another mystical layer, as Paul seems driven there to initiate a confrontation between the Counterfeit seed of the Fallen One and the Genuine Blood Heir of the Priesthood!

Interestingly, Shaul comes from the שאל, sha'al, root, the same as Sheol – hell, the Pit. Saul was a Benjamite – A figurative 'Son of the Right Hand' and self-proclaimed 'Pharisee of Pharisees'. In support of our position, Yahshua admonishes an entire group as Blind Pharisees! (Matthew 23:26) [Scales on their eyes perhaps] Most relate modern Haredim Jews – Ultra Orthodox to the ancient sect of Pharisees. Could they, like their counterparts of Yahshua's day pursue the rigors of tradition more than the Truth?

This root found in Pharisee is פרש, paras, which speaks of a sudden bursting forth of something that was previously well concealed! *This same root can also mean a 'horseman' as in horseman of the apocalypse!* Moreover, the Pey-Resh- Samech root also gives us Persia – reminding us of their King Cyrus who gave instructions to rebuild the Temple! Can you see where this link is taking us? Is there a connection to the restoration of this 'lost at Sea-dead' Levitical system and temple and these apocalyptic horsemen mentioned in Revelation who will seek to enthrone the Anti-Messiah and bring corrupt DNA to a false Altered ALTAR?

In summation, the 2nd Beast - Behemoth forms a compound Bet-Hey as in Bohu – empty, desolation; While Mem-Vav-Tav gives us Mut-Death. Again, Yahshua exposes this same group as "Whited Sepulchers, full of dead men's bones"!

Now, Back to the 6th Plague: Boils and Blains?

Exodus 9:8,9 And the LORD said unto Moses and unto Aaron, Take to you handfuls of ashes of the furnace, and let Moses sprinkle it toward the heaven in the sight of Pharaoh.

There are two ways to look at this 6th plague: Natural occurrences as a result of the spread of contagion as Ashes are released into the atmosphere and of course, the spiritual side.

The first anomaly found here is in what seems a redundant use of words in the Hebrew text and translated into the plural in English as 'handfuls'. The words translated for handfuls are: H#4393, מלא, melo, that which fills, fullness of the hands and H#2651, חפן, chophen, hollow of the hand.

The word melo is cognate with male` and millu, both hinting at a full judgment, a harvest, an ordination or consecration. Chophen is much harder to trace as its root is uncertain. However, we can see the Chet-Pey cognate of Kaf – the palm or hollow of the hand. Further, the Chet hints at a fence or boundary, a DNA helix, while Pey-Nun represents a 'form' or kind, a species.

It seems here that in this 6th plague a DIVINE WRATH is being released upon those who would oppose YHVH! He will judge without measure those who cross the DNA boundaries established by Him in Genesis 1 & 2. Those who are hybridized, whether by literal DNA manipulation or even more importantly, those who by reason of rebellion, harden their hearts resulting in a Hybridized Spirit! Once DNA is altered/altared it cannot be changed back without YHVH's intervention!

You have to come out of Babylon, you have to come out of the SEA and Stand upon the LAND! Think you can procrastinate much longer?

> Revelation 10:5,6 *And the angel which I saw stand upon the sea and upon the earth/land lifted up his hand to heaven. And sware by Him that liveth for ever and ever, who created heaven, and the things that therein are, and the earth, and the things that therein are, and the sea, and the things which are therein, that there should be time no longer:*

A Timely Illustration of That Wrath

Few would argue that the Outcasts of Israel are being gathered from among the Nations. Further, it is impossible to trace the DNA of individual tribal affiliations. Because that DNA has been compromised – raped by the Nations and forced into hiding until such time as Abba reveals! No Hebrew Roots or Messianic would argue the importance of the 12-Sons of Israel and their respective houses as it relates to tribal affiliation! Yet, everyone overlooks the only Daughter of Jacob – דינה, Dinah! This name indicates, judgment, retribution, an accounting. For reference, look at Genesis 34:1-31. I believe there's a connection to DNA and DINA-H, pointing to the DNA of YHVH!

In this text we find Shechem, Son of Hamor/Chamor the Hivite, sexually compromises Dinah.

**Note the Names:

- Shechem, H#7927 שכם

    Referred to as the shoulders, i.e. responsibility, to consent.

- Hamor, H#2544 חמור *Chamowr*

    Rendered as 'donkey' or ass; it also indicates that which is red, a euphemism for blood.

- Hivite, H#2340 חוי *Chivviy*

    It is derived from the root of H#2332, חוה, Chavvah – Eve! Life-giver, to live, cause to live!

From the entire account we can see that the Daughter of Jacob – DINA-H The DNA of YHVH – Just like Chavvah - was sexually raped in the hopes of gaining legal consent for the Enemy to Raise Up Another Bloodline by joining the 2 houses of the Hivite and Israel! The Counterfeit and the Genuine! Ironically, some presume that the child of this rape later became known as Asenath, the Wife of Joseph in Egypt!

It is this Asenath (Whom Abarim Publications says is a compound of 'Healed from harm' and storehouse and which, is related to Asinah or thorn bush – as in Sinai) and Joseph (Yah will do again) who will produce Ephraim and Manasseh: Translated as H#669, אפרים, meaning doubly fruitful and ASH HEAP. While Manasseh, H#4519, מנשה, is translated 'causing to forget'.

However, the Mem prefix of Menashe indicates 'from or out of', while the Nashe root hints at a loan being paid off, a memory forgotten or changed. This latter-day group will arise out of this

Plague of Boils and Blains – FROM the Ashes that are scattered upon the earth and having their minds renewed – SEALED – their slavery forgotten, their SEA DEBTS paid off, they will become doubly fruitful!

Boils and Blains
In Summation

- Boils, H#7822   שחין   *Shakiyn*

  It is translated as 'to burn'. It connotes leprosy as well. The root stem Shin-Chet, seach, relates to the mind or thoughts in one's conscious. It has a gematria of 368, the same as H#4285, מחשך, maksak; a hiding place, secrecy. Mahsak is the etymological root of Mask!

- Blains, H#76   אבעבעת   *Ababuot*

  From ababuah, to belch forth, erupt. As an inflammatory pustule. This word's origin is debated. The Alef-Bet-Ayin root is related to searching, looking for that which is cut off. It is related to Peah, the corner of a field, the forehead! While the Bet-Ayin-Tav root hints at a terror!

Did you note the inference to the forehead, the place of sealing, the mind that must be renewed else 'Men's hearts fail them for fear' as shown in:

> Luke 21:26 *Men's hearts failing them for fear, and for looking after those things which are coming on the earth: for the powers of heaven shall be shaken.*

The above Greek phrase 'looking after' is from the root of G#4328 pros-dok-ah'o, and indicates mental direction, thus a contemplative mind. The Mind's gateway is going to be opened at the release of these Beasts and those who are not sealed will be found in jeopardy!

Both words hint at far more than just open pustules or blisters. During the Exodus encounter, this plague was so horrific that even Pharaoh's magicians were unable to stand before Moshe! Medical research of diseases and their Physical side effects connects the symptoms with an aerosolized anthrax type, cancer causing respiratory agent whose carcinogens leach through the skin! It is deadly contagious and can be spread from man to beast! It is specific to CATTLE! By the way, the root of vaccine is vacca-cattle! By chance, the property owned by the Queen of England through her Salvage Claims on all the birth certificates of those lost at SEA is ironically referred to as – Chattel - Cattle!

Chapter 6

The 7th Plague: Grievous Hail[16]

Exodus 9:14-35

As we continue our study on these 'Plagues of the Greater Exodus', before the release of yet another plague (The seventh) we see that Pharaoh *has his heart hardened by YHVH* after refusing to let Israel go. We will address this position concisely,

---

[16] Sabine Alex http://www.torah-illustrations.blogspot.com/
Used with permission.

in a simple view from a New Testament perspective that I find also providing an assessment of the current condition of the hearts of many today. We will examine this point regarding 'heart condition' to give perspective before looking at the 7th plague!

> 2Thessalonians 2:10-12 *And with all deceivableness of unrighteousness in them that perish; because they received not the love of the truth that they might be saved. And* **for this cause YHVH shall send them strong delusion**, *that they should believe a lie: That they all might be damned who believed not the truth, but had pleasure in unrighteousness.*

In plain English: You cannot rebuke this one! Why? YHVH sends it! On to the 7th plague: Please note this phrase in Hebrew: *And hardened YHVH Pharaoh's heart.* As his heart is hardened, the people's hearts are synchronously also hardened! Now you can understand the pure insanity that seems to grip our present society! Pay attention here to the nuances found in the Hebrew text of: '*And hardened YHVH Pharaoh's heart...*'

ויחזק יהוה את-לב, v'yekzaq YHVH Et-lev - has a value of 590, the same as the phrase: Natan Melek. Natan indicates the exchange of tangible property, while Melek means king.

To put this into context, at the timing of the Exodus plagues there is a literal exchange of Kings [with their chattel] taking place in the Heavenlies as the Zodiacal precession moves from the House of the Bull-Shor, to that of Aries. Most scholars associate Aries with the Ram, but its Original depiction was that of The Man – The Shepherd-King! In retrospect, the condition of one's heart exposes the King who sits on its Throne!

What seems overlooked here as we consider the above - 'hearts' condition' is that it results from the consequence of disobedience: I. E. *A hardened heart!* Notice – the root of v'yekzaq – is H#2388, חזק, Chazak, and how it is presently translated here as 'harden', yet is more often rendered as 'strong or to repair'. This tells us that YHVH could have just as easily, strengthened and repaired the heart of Pharaoh, instead of hardening it, had Pharaoh responded in obedience! *Think about this if you continue to indulge in closet sin...A* hardened heart could very well be the worst of all plagues!

In reflection, the gematria of Chazak is 115, the same as Sinah, the root of Sinai, as in Mt. Sinai, where Israel, shortly after leaving Egypt, is offered an opportunity to have their Hearts *Repaired - Transformed* from the generational bonds of slavery!

Note Romans 12:2 *And be not conformed to this* **world*: but be ye transformed by the renewing of your mind, that ye may prove what is that good, and acceptable, and perfect, will of YHVH.* Based on our observations at Sinai, and being context-aware, it is the VOICE OF YHVH, which transforms Israel! How? By renewing their Minds! Yet, unfortunately as with many today, and as in this case, Israel doesn't want to hear, sending Moshe instead!

Hence, Romans 12 is significant to our study as it finishes a powerful thought broken up by the textural division from the previous chapter 11 which explains what world we are not to conform to!

> Romans 11:1,4 *I say then, Hath YHVH cast away His People? Yah forbid. For I am also an Israelite, of the Seed of Abraham, the tribe of Benjamin. Even so then at this present time there is also a REMNANT according to the election of grace!*

How do we become a HEBRAIC remnant? This is the aim of a renewed mind.

Ergo, the Enemy would have you believe that there is NO

REMNANT, i.e. a True, non –GMO seed of YHVH! But even now we are being gathered from the four corners of the world! This 7th Plague will expose the Remnant and their Counterfeits! Dear Reader! It has always been about the war between the Serpent and the SEED of YHVH! One Seed will have their hearts/mind seared, hardened, the other will be Transformed by renewing their minds!

Likewise, it is the Remnant being gathered, who, after having their mind Transformed - renewed - will prove the will of YHVH. The Greek word for Prove is Gk.#1381, dokemazo, rendered 'to test', examine, and scrutinize, to recognize something as genuine after examination! This tells us only a renewed mind can demonstrate the power of His Word. Transformed here in the Greek is Gk.#3339, Me-ta-mor-fo-o, to change into another form and is first seen when Yahshua is transfigured on the Mountain!

**Remember the word 'MIND'! This is significant because heart and mind from a Hebraic perspective are synonymous. Each of these horrific incidents of a future plague will indeed molest the hearts and minds of those who are not sealed by the Spirit of Elohiym! With this in mind, please pay heed to this short aside regarding *plagues upon the heart…*

Plagues Upon the Heart…

Having clearly said as much in the Hebrew text, though it is not noticed at all in the KJV English, there is, nonetheless, for those who dig deeper, a transformation seen taking place in the text that tells us each successive 7th through 10th plague tests the hearts of those affected by it! Consequently, the subtle change in the text in verse 14 becomes an eye-opener as we contemplate a future of plagues: *For I will at this time send all my plagues upon thine heart, and upon thy servants, and upon thy people; that thou mayest know that there is none like me in all the earth.*

Why Would YHVH Specifically Reference 'Plagues Upon the Heart'?

In answer, I want to call attention to those two highlighted words: *Plagues* & *Heart*; plagues H#4046, is written as מגפה, maggafah and blandly translated here as plague, although that by itself, it is a somber warning. On the other hand, its root – nagad, comes from the Nun-Gimmel – root; which hints at, 'that which is before', in front of, much like an image or likeness in front of you. It also points toward striking, touching, INFECTING, etc.

What do you think is really taking place? To put it bluntly, like Adam, You as a person spoke into existence what is standing before you! Once that becomes a reality, you then impregnate your personal creation and your circumstances by continuing to speak to it! In simple laymen's terms "you are thus creating generational offspring"! Therefore, the language we speak is critical to changing our DNA! In other words, you are, what you say! For this reason I believe it is imperative to take advantage of the only time in created history to have access, with relative ease to the Creator's Language – Hebrew! WE

MUST LEARN TO SPEAK THIS NEW LANGUAGE! Why? ENGLISH IS THE LANGUAGE OF SLAVERY! If you look closely at some of the older Black's Law Dictionaries you'll find such examples: Human = monster, male/female are simply beast/animal terms, birth/berth certificates, licenses, law vs. statute, Mister, Ma'am, Sir, liberty instead of freedom etc. All are terms dealing with those enslaved by the Elite!

As we continue looking at the word plague – maggafah and its root nagad, this may seem off beat, but the first time the Nun-Gimmel-Dalet word is used is in describing the

Woman – Ishah, who is brought before – nagad, the Man – Ish.

**Remember! At Creation's inception, Adam was a Nephesh Chai – A Speaking Soul – He spoke - called every living creature into existence.

**See Genesis 2:19 – including his helpmeet, the woman, whom, afterward, YHVH Elohiym forms with His own hands!

Adam was created to be the Manifest Voice of YHVH seen in the earth realm! As the representative of YHVH in the Earth, he walked in both Spirit and Natural realms! With the physical restrictions of today, we must ask ourselves what allowed this? I believe simply because Adam represented the Living Tabernacle! Following this pattern, after the fall, the wilderness Tabernacle is set in Adam's fallen image and thus, depicted with an alienated Mind – one that could no longer transcend both Spirit and Natural world. Therefore The Holiest of Holies of that Wilderness Tabernacle which was found housing the Presence/Mind/Voice of YHVH only lamentably represented Fallen Mans restricted ability to be in His Presence and allowed his solitary access to this place once per year!

Once access was denied because of sin, Adam only lived in the fleshly realm! The Law of Sin and Death is now working in him. But the law of the spirit of life in Messiah Yahshua frees us from death – allowing access to both realms again. How? Note the prototype of Genesis 2, as it pertains to Eve (Chavah) in relationship to Adam.

Once formed, she stands in front of him as an image or help meet in the English (KJV). In Hebrew you have עזר כנגדו, Ezer k'negdo. A Waiting Womb! She didn't look like him quite obviously, so how could she be his image? Bear in mind, Adam was only a vessel, *a light sac* - filled with the Voice. This Voice transferred DNA from the Creator out of the spiritual ADAMAH to the natural realm of the Earth-Eretz! In hindsight, it would seem there has to be a gateway, a curtain or veil between the two allowing access or denying it! Just like the firmament between the heavens!

In this regard, could this future 7th plague also see this Edenic gateway opened for the Remnant? Those Outcasts are called Hebrews – those who have crossed over - allowing them once again to have access to the Holiest of Holies, their minds transformed, becoming NEW – and found housing the Word which will give them knowledge, wisdom, understanding, direction, Authority, and Power, as well as, the ability to transcend physiological supernatural boundaries (not be bound by time and space) while the future Harlot and her paramour, the Anti-Messianic Pharaoh are subjected to abject confusion, fear, depression, miscommunication, etc.!

The above was only ever possible in Adam and Eve's (Chavah) capacity as ONE – ECHAD, the condition where his seed is planted in her womb and then produces ONE in his image! They were intended to exist as ONE – ECHAD in the Mind first, not the flesh! Being able to speak creation into existence, they have a mandate: To Produce Sons of Elohiym – (See Genesis 1:28) who will be fruitful, multiply, replenish the earth, subdue it and have dominion over the SEA – AIR – EARTH! This is intriguing as these areas are to this day, the places of dominion for the Fallen Ones! I contend that YHVH knew in advance what was going to happen and made plans to produce Sons who would replenish, H#4390, מלא, ma'la, to be filled, be armed, to mass themselves against another! The Battle is coming – But be aware - the Battlefield is in the Mind first!

These same letters above, מלא only read this time in reverse, are seen in Isaiah 53:7 in a mistranslated, misunderstood word: It says Yahshua was *like a sheep before her shearers;* hinting of a weakness, the inability to remedy one's situation. However, the Hebrew word used in the text for 'dumb', to be silent, and found with reversed letters is – אלם, 'alam. As such, it is powerfully indicating that He, Messiah chose at that specific time to withhold His VOICE because He has a mission, one at which

Adam failed! Having conquered the Powers of the Eretz – Land, He is going to descend into the SEA - underworld, then ascend through the Air and destroy the Powers who occupied those realms!

From Genesis 3 forward, until the coming of Messiah that Voice had previously been on the other side of the Doorway – The Veil! Yet, He destroyed that Veil! The Holy of Holies is now accessible! Incidentally, the English phrase Holy of Holies in Hebrew is – Qodesh h'qadashim – however, the same location is also referred to as the H'DEBIR – THE SANCTUARY OF HIS WORD VOICE!

Oddly enough, as we continue looking at Eve (Chavah) as the help meet of Adam, again, translated in Hebrew as Ezer k'negdo whose numeric value is 360, (Which is the same as the Hebrew word mesek, a Seed Pouch used by one sowing seed) we find that 360 is also cognate with Mem-Shin-Chet – Mashiach – The Anointed One! Following that line of thinking, then The Last Adam – Yahshua was Himself a Vocal Seed Pouch! After much thought, the connection between Plague – maggafah and Nagad is compelling! Consider this, if there is a genuine article, person or a place created by YHVH, naturally the enemy always attempts a counterfeit. If this is true, then perhaps maybe we should consider the following of his first con-jobs!

The Counterfeit Woman - Ishah – Ezer K'negdo

Could this possibly be saying that the counterfeit ISHAH – WOMAN known simply as the future Harlot of Babylon, is in fact an alias of the future Religious Church – and that she has been formed as a copy to the genuine Eve? Her role this time to function as a counterfeit that will operate as The Ezer K'negdo Who Stands Before Pharaoh! She will serve as Pharaoh, the Anti-Messiah's Womb even as Eve was to Adam! I firmly believe it is She - The Counterfeit who will be stricken with this

7th – Plague! YOU MAKE THE CALL! After all, Revelation 18:4 tells us if we don't come out, we will partake of her plagues!

Though you remain skeptical, the enemy has not changed his method of operation. From Genesis 3 forward this is why you see the identical results between seed lines as found in Genesis 3:15 where the Serpent's Seed and Adam's seed are both in the womb and a subsequent war between the seed lines began. Please remember: Cain vs. Abel, Isaac vs. Ishmael, Jacob vs. Esau, Moshe vs. Pharaoh, David vs. Saul, Solomon vs. Absalom, Yahshua vs. Barabbas!

That is why, in our text YHVH is presenting a Paternity Suit, a lawful claim against Pharaoh for the sons and daughters of Israel – ZION - HIS FIRSTBORN – who will be distinguished from the Scion of Pharaoh by that produced in the womb – heart! This 7th Plague presents this Paternity Suit again, calling forth those Sons of Elohiym who will subdue the SEA – AIR – and LAND - Eretz! At Yahshua's Miqveh (baptism) John is heard saying: *This is My Beloved Son – Hear Him – The Voice!* Will you, the Sons of Israel, the Sons of Elohiym who were once Outcasts now come forth and be heard as well?

By the way, Scion is the English derivative of Zion – the place where two separate branches are grafted together! In the natural, they must have similar DNA like Ephraim and Judah! Light and darkness cannot dwell together, like wheat and tares it takes threshing – plaguing to expose the SEED! This is why the enemy wants to comingle his seed with Man's, so that YHVH cannot eradicate him without destroying His own! As a point of fact, He denies the existence of a **remnant** that has uncompromised DNA! But, I contend, there is indeed a remnant! Praise HIM!

Once again, as we continue, please note what is said regarding The Harlot of Revelation 17:3 ...*I saw a woman sit upon a scarlet colored beast*... This woman is, to put it plainly, a whore.

Further, to add clarity, the Greek word for beast, Gk.#2342, tha-re-on, can mean a brutal, savage, MAN KILLER. Now, pay attention to what ancient Greek Mythology has to say, specifically as it relates to their gods Europa and Zeus-The Bull; the former being the goddess who became his consort after Zeus changes himself into a white bull.

For context, this Bull represents the Ancient House of Pharaoh whose name is translated as 'His Great House', yet carries the Pey-Resh root indicating a 'Bull'. Like Zeus, Pharaoh thought to have Israel as his consort! In our day, He carries her out to SEA (Admiralty law) where he impregnates her. She rides him, a euphemism for sexual acts - upon the SEA! Those born out of the Union upon the SEA are her offspring! Hence, the imperative! Come out of her my People! The birth/berth certificate identifies you as the lost at Sea - Child of Pharaoh! Retrospectively, the Egyptians' believed that Pharaoh became Osiris – The deity who was both Fertility God as well as, The God of the Dead!

Moreover, the Harlot of Revelation is also said to be *'that great city who has dominion over the kings of the earth'* Revelation 17:18. Prevailing arguments here point at both Rome and Jerusalem as the seat of 2 of the great Triad of religions who must be purged before YHVH visits the iniquity of the World! However, the 3rd, England sits at the top of this list too! The Great Harlot of Babylon could indeed be a future figurehead Queen of England!

FYI: There are two separate, functioning Crowns in England: One being the Queen, Elizabeth II. Although great wealth and power is hers, she functions largely in a ceremonial role and serves to deflect attention away from the other Crown, who issues her marching orders, by controlling the Parliament. This Crown is made up of a committee of 12 banks led by the Bank of England (The House of Rothschild). They in turn, rule from the 677-acre, independent sovereign state known as The City of

London, or simply "The City". It is not part of England proper, just as Washington D.C. is not part of the United States, but is rather, an integral part of the corporation UNITED STATES OF AMERICA!

What is fascinating, though not coincidental, is the number 677, which has the gematria of a unique Hebrew phrase: מצרי שאול, Mitsri Sheol – translated as 'The straits or fortress of death'! Further, Mitsri is the root of Mitsrayim – Egypt! For this reason, The Son(s) of YHVH went down into Egypt for a season – to break free from this curse!

To add further emphasis, an entire continent is named after the Harlot riding the Beast! That harlot is Europa: which is said to originate from the ערב, Erev root (Ernest Kline's dictionary) indicating, that which declines, enters into, to change, barter, take on an obligation or debt, to become mixed or confused. It is also the root of the word describing the 4th plague of Great Swarms – Arov – wild beasts/Chimera! Indeed! There are many voices (Mixed-confused-Babel) in the world…

Even today the Hebrew rendering of Europa is Europe, אירופה, Europah, a compound meaning – owr, to illustrate, shed light and Peh – mouth! It has the same value as the Hebrew word H#1300, ברק, baraq and meaning lightening (Think Mt. Sinai). Europa – the Babylon – Babel/confused Harlot, the counterfeit also known as the Ezer K'negdo she too has a voice! Like Ishah, the woman – Eve, she instead carries the Voice or Seed of Pharaoh – Zeus, the Bull! Making the Voice of Pharaoh, synonymous with the voice of the future Anti-Messiah! Can you recognize that voice? On the other hand, Yahshua says, *"My sheep know my voice and another they will not follow!"*

**Remember the above word baraq!

As we return to our discussion of YHVH now turning the plagues upon Pharaoh and Egypt's heart, let's move on to consider a different perspective of this 2nd word – heart. The Hebrew has it H#3820, לב, this word lev is again, rather weakly translated heart here by the KJV translators. Accordingly, if we're not careful, we will find ourselves in their condition, our thoughts limited, as without exclusion the Western mind associates this word heart - with the literal organ called the heart, yet according to Dr. Eldon Clem, professor of Semitic languages at the Jerusalem University College, in all Semitic tongues without exception, *lev indicates the MIND* – the Womb or seat of our emotions that are, **simply the fetuses of the seed planted within!**

As we proceed, the Lamed – Bet root of Lev, whose value is 32 - hints at 'joined to', i.e. a Union. Thus, whatever we think, meditate upon, or reflect upon is what/with whom we are joined to; as in to be married/intimate with! These letters written in reverse are Bet – Lamed and give us Bel – Ba'al, the Babylonian deity-indicating a lord or husband!

This short foray into Exodus 9:14 and the language change tells us the 7th plague shifts focus and begins to refine the Lawful Declaration of Paternity for those 'First Born of YHVH' who would inherit the Land of the Living! Consequently, the Renewing of Our Mind is the 1st step out of Babylon! Coming out will be difficult once the 7th plague is released upon the Heart/Mind of Pharaoh and his SEED!

It is through the vehicle of these plagues that YHVH is going to cut off Pharaoh and his Babylonian Whore and their offspring: 'His' being – those belonging to him, Pharaoh. The Hebrew word for 'cut off' is H#3582, כחד, chahad, to hide, conceal, cut off, and to make desolate; chahad's value is 32 the same as lev. Is YHVH about to 'cut off' their hearts?

Perhaps causing their hearts to fail as in Luke 21:26 where men's hearts are seen failing them for fear? Let me again remind you of the admonition given us in Revelation 18:4: Come out of her my

People! If we do, we need not fear the coming plagues! They serve a purpose separating Wheat from Tares! As we continue looking further, the individual word pictures of the letters of Chahad – כחד, to hide or conceal, will reveal each their individual mysteries and add clarity themselves! Kaf-Chet-Dalet.

Kaf, whose value is 20, (esriym) represents authority, it signifies a 'title deed' Vis a Vis, ownership! Kaf is related to Keter – כתר, crown. Kaf's value, 20 - esriym is styled עשרים, and like Keter/crown also has the same value 620! Lawfully, the title deed requires a SEAL; the Seal is placed upon the Crown-Forehead-MIND, the seat of the Man's Authority! Are you beginning to connect the dots? The Sealing of Mankind is coming!

Continuing, the Chet indicates a fence, a boundary as in a DNA boundary, while the Dalet represents a door! Whoever is allowed access to the door of our minds will cross over the threshold or boundary and assume title deed to our lives!

Now you understand a bit more regarding:

> Revelation 9:4 *And it was commanded them that they should not hurt the grass of the earth, neither any green thing, neither any tree: but only those men which have not the seal of YHVH in their foreheads.*

The Greek word for foreheads is *'met-o-pon'* and comes from the Hebrew word מצח, metsach. Once more, as we break the word apart, the Mem indicating a womb or place of origin, while the root stem Tzade-Chet gives us words that indicate an exposed or barren place, something clear or dazzling. It carries the ability to express thoughts without stuttering or hesitation! Consider this, the EMF – electromagnetic frequencies - and their assault on the Pineal gland with their subliminal messages have the ability to disable your innate power to think cogent thoughts and thus, blur the distinction between good and evil – in effect -

Turning off the 'God-Gene'! Is it possible that YHVH sends this strong delusion to exacerbate this condition Himself? He did say He would send such! Beware dear Reader and prepare accordingly!

Moving along, we find that the Tzade-Chet root stem is also the root of Isaac, H#3327, יצחק, rendered 'laughter' a root which expresses an attitude toward something claimed, but seemingly impossible to realize! This is why Sarah laughed!

Sealing the foreheads of the Remnant will enable us to *'call those things which are not as though they were',* creating with our words before seeing them in the physical realm! This was the Power inherent in the original Adamic - Altar - being able to procreate with the Language of Creation – bringing forth Sons in the Image of Elohiym! The obverse of this is to be sealed in the forehead by the Anti-Messiah and produce sons of Belial!

Grievous Hail, or Was It?

If the aforementioned is true, i.e. there is link between heart and mind, and if indeed, there are Spiritual and Physical 'side effects' to this plague, then how did the Grievous Hail effect the Hearts of Pharaoh, his people, and the cattle that had been stalled in barns having survived the previous plagues? Subsequently, how will the Plague of Hail described in Revelation affect us?

**See Revelation 16:18-21. The text of Exodus should explain! Let's examine Exodus 9:15-35:

Frankly, I was curious when I first saw the text here in Exodus 9 verse 15 where YHVH says He will smite Pharaoh and his people with pestilence, because of the use of the Hebrew word H#1698, דבר: deber, defined as 'a destroying word'. Its cognate languages root hint at setting things in a row, arranging them in order and to subdue. This pestilence will cut off Pharaoh from the earth, which is a phrase indicating to conceal or make desolate as in removing the remembrance of his lineage or seed! There will be no seed line left! Is this akin to the reverse effect of those who're the Sons of Elohiym that are seen being restored to their Edenic Seed line of the Last Adam?

The phrase 'thou shalt be cut off' in Hebrew is styled: ותכחד: V'tichad and has a value of 438, the same as the phrase עצר לחם, 'atsar lechem. 'Atsar means to shut up, to restrain, keep in slavery, make barren, and total rejection – while lechem is the Hebrew word for bread, as in the bread of His Presence! YHVH will cut off His Presence – a famine of His Word that ultimately leads to great destitution. As a result of this famine, for most, nothing grows and neither is the INTENDED seed for the next year's crop produced: But what of the Remnant? The answer is found written to encourage us in:

> Psalms 37:25 *I have been young, and now am old; yet have I not seen the righteous forsaken, nor his SEED begging BREAD!*

In a famine that which is beneficial is not produced - yet, alas, something does grow! According to Genesis 3:18 …thorns and thistles are produced…the phrase thorns and thistles is written: H#6975, H#1863, וקוץ ודרדר V'Qowts v'dardar. Qowts is a word taken again, from the idea of 'cutting off' like Pharaoh is cut off, while Dardar, repeats the Hebrew word for generation – Dor! After the Fall, the Ground – The Adamah Altar would no longer produce Seed in the Image of YHVH until Messiah Yahshua restores it, the Ground – Adamah!

From Genesis 3 Adam is cut off from the Voice -The Seed! There is a veil between the 2 worlds – Spirit and Flesh – The Fleshly or Carnal man can see and hear the Voice on the other side but, has limited understanding! The Wilderness Tabernacle was a shadow picture of this! The Heart/MIND of Adam was cut off – a veil separated the Holiest of Holies – The Mind whose light was turned off in Genesis 3. However, Yahshua breaks down this Partition – the result is that now we can have the mind of Messiah – allowing us to walk after the spirit, not after the flesh! Belatedly, the 3rd-Temple will have NO ARK OF THE COVENANT – thus, NO MIND – No Heart, like Dorothy's Tin Man – the 1st fictional Hybridized Chimera! Oh, yes! You should stop here and revisit that old movie! The Elite Powers used their magic incantations in many of these videos to pass their coded messages to those initiated and to further enslave those who're not!

V'Qowts v'dardar has a value of 616, the same as the phrase: Manat Cuwsiym - The Cup of their Portion! Each man is made to drink from this cup until Messiah comes who drinks it without sin! That number 616 is also the value of התורה, h'torah. The anti-type of the Torah – lawlessness - is the counterfeit Cup being offered by Babylon the Harlot! She is going to rebuild the 3rd – Temple and in doing so, put up another VEIL denying her followers the access to a renewed Mind!

As we continue, Amos 8:11 tells of this *'famine of hearing the words of YHVH'*. This doesn't mean the complete absence of His Word, only that most areas will not have it available! YHVH is capable of sending Quail and Manna to His Remnant! For example: There has been a FAMINE OF TRUTH in the pulpits for a generation! If you want to survive - **Find out where the Word or Seed is being sown and move there now!**

Incidentally, the Hebrew word for famine, H#7458, רעב, ra`ab, has the same root letters (As we've shown) as seen in Europa, remember this Greek goddess? That root is ערב, Erev, a root (Ernest Kline) indicating, that which declines, enters into, to change, barter, to take on an obligation or debt, to become mixed or confused, also as in Arab. The Famine will cause many to enter into contract with Europa, the goddess upon the SEA!

Equally, it is the same root letters as Ayin-Bet-Resh - EBER –

Hebrew, One who stands in opposition to another, one who crosses over. This is reminiscent of the ladder or stairway, upon which, we may cross over in order to hear The Voice of YHVH. This ladder or stairway is nothing short of the Mind of Yahshua! LET THIS MIND BE IN YOU! Can you say amen?

This is what becoming a Hebrew means, walking in the spirit with a renewed mind, having crossed over the veil of the flesh! Abraham by faith walked here, so did Moshe and others, yet for those who did not, the voice could be seen, heard, but not understood! Yahshua was the Living Voice who spoke, He was heard in parabolic form, until He opened the MINDS and the understanding of His disciples!

Moreover, EBER – the plural being Ivrit, Hebrews - those who have 'crossed over' – their minds being renewed - will have BREAD – though quite possibly, Europa and ערב – Europe and Arabia, along with those who say they are Hebrews and are not will experience this FAMINE! What about the UNITED STATES OF AMERICA? Let me show you this in Hebrew. No other language will reveal this to you.

ארצות הברית של אמריקה Artsot haberiyt shel America – Which is literally translated: The Covenant Lands of America. Its value of 1900 is the same as this verse in Job 34:27 *Because they turned back from him, and would not consider any of his ways:* Consider is the Hebrew word שכל, sakal, to be prudent, consider wisely, and to comprehend! Sakal has a gematria of 350, the same as natsar, to guard, watch, and keep secret, to preserve, to block or keep from others! Why is this important? Let's get a history lesson.

Many Scholars believe that America's etymology came from Machir, the 1st born of Manasseh. Many also believe that the aboriginal natives were from the Tribe of Manasseh with Ephraim migrating here later! Machir is a sobering word meaning 'Sold', while Manasseh indicates a forgetting, as in a debt paid off! Though sold into slavery by EUROPA – and Berthed/Born out of the SEA an opportunity for expunging that debt by coming out of BABYLON IS OFFERED – YET - America will be CUT OFF FOR THEIR REBELLION! Though a Remnant will be saved! As of the writing of this paragraph 4/27/21 there has never been a more rebellious populace in this country aside perhaps from what is often called the Great Rebellion or The Civil War! Prepare yourself dear Reader!

Chapter 7

Who Exactly Is Cut Off?

As we take a short detour here let me ask you a rather simple question? Did YHVH lie with the statement regarding the cutting off of Pharaoh? To some it may seem so, because Pharaoh and Egypt are NOT totally CUT OFF – the closest thing to their being cut of is in the 10th plague where the 1st-Born dies! What's more, YHVH said the plagues would be upon their hearts/minds. Yet, here it seems we see physical devastation. Was this a literal or figurative plague? Let's highlight some familiar descriptions for understanding.

- YHVH sent thunder and hail with fire which rained upon the land (Verse 23).

- Hail smote throughout Egypt all that was in the field, man and beast. Every herb was smote and every tree was broken. (Verse 24).

- Goshen had no hail. (Verse 31).

- Flax and barley smitten. (Verse 32).

- Thunder is from H#6963, קול, voice, proclamation, and thunderings. To call aloud, to Sing or Shout! Hmmmm?

Sound familiar? This precedent first happened in Genesis 3:8 when the VOICE called unto Adam, who had hid himself – after being cut off - from the Paniym – face of His Presence! The Voice was the Menorah – The Fire of YHVH – the Ish Man!

This Thundering Voice of Fire now is seen walking in the garden amongst the Trees! Because Adam's Mind was straightaway in a corrupt state he could see and hear the voice but COULD NOT COMPREHEND Him – so, like Israel at Sinai he hides or withdraws himself! As with Israel at Sinai, Yahshua came to renew his mind, but Adam chose to clothe himself instead in the flesh! That's why they were put out of Eden away from the Tree of Life! Had they been allowed to stay, their flesh could have lived, but their minds were corrupted!

This is the same creative scenario as seen in Genesis 2:6 where Fire and Water and the Voice of YHVH detonated in the Gan-garden of Eden! An explosion of Creative power causing the First Born of YHVH to be formed – ADAM! Thinking back, do you remember what it was that The Voice in the garden called to Adam?

'And He said: Adam where are you'? ויאמר לו איכה, vayomer lo ayyehcah. You can spot *'and he said'* from the Hebrew 'vayomer' easily. Next, Lo, can be rendered 'NO or Not' while ayyehcah, is translated as 'where, or whence' and actually comes from אין, ah'yin, meaning faileth, fatherless, incurable, empty, a vacuum. Further, the Alef-Yod root indicates habitable. I believe what Yahshua – The Voice, is declaring in the Midst of Fire and Wind (The Cool/Ruach of the day) is that in his current position Adam's mind is not tenantable by the Voice, and as a result, must be renewed! No Voice or Seed is there, he is Fatherless, empty, for all intents and purposes he is cut off: But, he will NOT be left that way! Now, let's proceed with our above examples.

- Hail, H#1259   ברד   *Barad*

    The Hebrew is barad, and is translated by the KJV as 'hail'. Yet, it is also found styled as Barod (different vowels) in Genesis 31:10 where the flock of Jacob is separated from that of his father-in-law Laban. Jacob institutes a unique method through what we now see as a type of DNA manipulation whereby his flock is separated after having become ringstraked, speckled, and grisled – BAROD, i.e. multicolored, as in a variegated garment, in other words, they were marked! Hence, this very reason of separating him from his brothers, we see Joseph is later given a variegated Coat of Colors! Consequently, he will be scattered, separated (Marked so that only YHVH can identify him) into the Nations and will be of many colors!

Similarly, it seems this Barad or plague of hail upon Egypt was sent to sever between the DNA of the House of Jacob and the DNA of the House of Pharaoh! Let me fallback and explain a bit...

In the chapter previous to Genesis 31 we see Jacob placing 'pilled Rods' in front of his flock for them to SEE – Pilled is from H#6478, פצל, patsal, to peel. The letter Pey represents the Mouth; a place of speaking, while the Tzade-Lamed root gives us 'image', shadow, and likeness. 'Rods' is from H#4731, מקל, maqqel, indicating to germinate. As we dissect the word, the Mem of maqqel indicates a womb; the Qof-Lamed root gives us Qowl – voice! What we find is that Jacob knew there was power in the spoken word from the earlier encounter with the Voice or DNA – at THE Sullam סלם – Ladder – a word which would in like manner, cause the Flock or House of Jacob/Israel to germinate! By the way, its value (Sullam) of 130 is the same as Sinai! Moreover, the phrase 'In front or before' is H#5526, נכח, nacah, meaning before, in front, but also straightforward *as in a legal case that must be amended*!

In view of these definitions, this 'Barad' – Hail seemingly, has the power to both procreate and destroy - effectively changing the DNA of those who will hear and those who won't! The Voice of YHVH is literally seen in the Form of an ethereal combination of Wind/Water - Mist/Fire that Egypt can only describe as HAIL WITH FIRE!

Now, prayerfully, you recall that YHVH declares He would send upon the heart/minds of Pharaoh and Egypt a pestilence called a plague H#1698, דבר, in Hebrew translated a 'deber' which we've shown to indicate the results of which, will cut off one seed, while setting another in order? Is it thus, an accident that this word for HAIL – BAROD, has the same letters as DEBER only arranged differently? Moreover, if we read Barod backwards: Dalet-Resh-Bet we have a word meaning a 'goad', to prod, to use words to incite! Once again, we 'see' a natural or supernatural phenomenon described from the purview of a sterile English KJV description, when in fact, the Hebrew reveals far more than just a fiery hailstorm!

Let's Take A Quick Look at Some Identical Events!

Our curious episode happens again at Sinai! Exodus 19:16,19-20:18. Where Israel SEES the Voice: Pay close attention! Especially where they 'see' thunderings and lightning. Once more…

- Lightning, H#1300   ברק   *Baraq*

    Remember its value of 302 is the same as אירופה, Europa to shed or release light from the mouth!

**Do you recall this ancient mythological Greek goddess?

If we rearrange the letters of baraq to form קרב, qerev, we have the idea of both a state of formal war being declared and a word which indicates the middle, midst, the seat of the emotions, the heart or mind! Like the edict given Adam, a declaration of formal war against the powers of the SEA, AIR and LAND at Mt. Sinai is taking place as the Sons of Elohiym stand before the Voice! Take a look at more of our key words from the Sinai encounter:

- Smoke, H#6225   עָשָׁן   ʿAshan

    It is smoke, to fume, and to be wroth or furious!

- Fire, H#784   אֵשׁ   ʿEsh

    It is fire, from the same root as MAN - אִישׁ!

The word play upon SEE – SEA is vital to understanding this next plague! Europa – the Whore of Babylon – gives birth-berth upon the SEE-SEA to Pharaoh! The Plague of Hail-Barad is sent to destroy this WOMB of water! A full-scale assault is launched upon the minds of those who are not SEALED - Sea-led - by the Mark or Tav-Sign of the Covenant of YHVH upon their foreheads! The world as we know it today has been in an uproar because of the potential of 5G and now 6G technologies and their capabilities to manipulate the minds/DNA of the people! But who can stand against the Power of His Voice?

What happens next at Sinai indicates that all Israel SAW & Heard the Voice – Qowl while the mountain was on fire, but few comprehended, hastily removing themselves in fear! What really happened? The Psalmist gives us a much more precise and vivid insight! Please see Psalms 29:1-11 which reveals that His Voice breaks the Cedars of Lebanon!

- Cedars, H#730   ארז   *Araz*

    It is defined as 'cedars', but is from the root indicating to CONTRACT ONESELF, TO MAKE A FIRM COMPACT! Its gematria of 208, is the same as Bet-Vav-Resh – בור, bowr, a pit, well or dungeon. The word describing the same pit whereat Joseph was stripped of his verse-colored coat of inheritance and thrown into for 3-days or figuratively, 3000 years! [A day is as 1000-years a 1000-years as a day Psalms 90:4, 2Peter 3:8]

Joseph is coming out of this well as we speak and this time, he will not be subject to Pharaoh, neither the jealous whims of his brothers! This end result of this plague is that it will nullify all contracts with the House of Pharaoh, setting in proper order, the House of Joseph!

Continuing, this Voice at Mt. Sinai causes the Hinds to calve! The word hinds, H#355, אילוה, 'ayalah, comes from an unused root, אול, uwl, meaning the belly as in a prominence, to twist, and also noble mighty men! The English word Calve is from H#2342, חול, chuwl, to dance, writhe, whirl, and be pained! This is figurative of the Time of Jacob's Troubles! The House of Jacob is hearing the word whose DNA causes birthing in the Mighty Men! How can men give Birth? By SPEAKING THE DABAR-WORD OF YHVH AND CREATING A HABITATION FOR THE KING!

> Jeremiah 30:7 *Alas! For that day is great, so that none is like it: it is even the time of Jacob's trouble; but he shall be saved out of it.*

Trouble, H#6869, is defined here as צרה, tsarah, meaning affliction, but it can also indicate a vexor wife!

I assume you did you notice the above phrase *'cedars of*

Lebanon"? Lebanon has the same root as Laban! With this plague, Jacob's contract with Laban is now formally broken. The irascible Laban deceived Jacob 10-times, switched daughters in marriage and attempts to keep all of Jacob's clan as his slaves! It is also notable that Laban lived in Padan Aram, which most scholars equate with the original Babylon – Chaldean area! Don't you see all these connections that link our future to these powerful prophetic shadow pictures? We will experience the contract with Babylon, our Laban, being broken as we determine to Come Out of Her my People!

Here is where things get interesting! The word Padan, of Padan Aram above, is the Hebrew H#6307, פדן, described by most as an obscure, debated root, with most haplessly saying it isn't Semitic and thus not originating from the Hebrew. Yet, it is seen in words like pedagogue, from a Greek Word indicating a slave who escorts a boy to school and back. It hints at an education directed towards children, it hints at setting a ransom, to be sold, to redeem. Infamously, it is also seen in the word pedophilia. Let that sink in as today's news is filled with tidings of the Babylonian Elite who are almost daily being exposed as pedophiles!

Continuing, the second word in Padan Aram is written ארם, pronounced Aram, and hints at that which is between, high or lofty, to divide! These are the same letters rearranged as אמר, omer, the word or thoughts of a person that become manifest or living! Laban attempts to enslave the House of Jacob by constantly exposing them to the slave's mentality, creating a culture of words whose educational system promotes bondage, the cruelest form of which is sexual perversion!

Again, as we write, a culture war exists over sexualized gender pronouns and anyone found using either subject to being categorized as misogynist or feminist and/or homophobic! Talk about the power to use words to dictate the course of a People! Wow!

In conclusion, as we finish looking at the 7th Plague, the similarities between this Powerful Manifestation occurring at Sinai and the Exodus plague of Hail differ only in whom it is directed toward and how it is used! For instance, the same word – דבר – Dabar can be a PROMISED WORD OR A PLAGUE! In fact, we see the Sinai event rehearsed again in Acts 2 where a Rushing Mighty Wind and Fire rests upon the Believers!

An epiphanic episode where, once again, we have the declaration of a Paternity Suit! The Messiah restored the Voice in the Earth bringing forth the Sons of Elohiym and He has restored the ability for our minds to be renewed in order to become the Temple of the Living Elohiym!

The 8th Plague: Locusts[17]
Exodus 10:3-20

---

[17] Sabine Alex http://www.torah-illustrations.blogspot.com/
Used with permission.

The Exodus Keys

It is our position, after dissecting the 7-previous plagues, let's endeavor to move forward in our discussion of whether or not YHVH has brought a Petition or Suit of Paternity against the House of Pharaoh and insisting that Israel, His first-born son be released. Set against the innocuous King James English background, Pharaoh is asked by the Creator in our above text (Exodus 10:3): *How long will you refuse to humble yourself before me?*

Let me pause here a moment. It is my humble opinion that the plagues have already begun and our lives are being affected on multiple levels. That being said, how befitting the current Season and its affected Peoples should be confronted by the admonishment of:

> 2Chronicles 7:14 *If my people, which are called by my name, shall humble themselves, and pray, and seek my face, and turn from their wicked ways; then will I hear from heaven, and will forgive their sin, and will heal their land.*

By the way, NO ONE comes out of Babylon or Egypt who fails in the above! How long will this rebellious generation flaunt its haughty attitude and put their collective thumbs in the eye of a Holy God? Look closer as we investigate a few key words in the text.

We will begin with the Hebrew word for humble, H#6031, ענה, pronounced `anah, and defined as 'humble', yet the root indicates a refusal to answer, to respond or to testify in a legal sense! Therefore, it could read: *"How long will you refuse to testify or respond before me?"* Even in a worldly court system, a court ordered paternity test couldn't be refused. If it is, the individual is held in contempt and fined. Pharaoh is going to answer one way or another shortly for his contempt of the Court and Judge of Creation!

Now, please note the word 'refuse' above: H#3985, translated in Hebrew as מאן, ma'en, and rendered of course, as 'refuse'. Though this word is placid in its English revelation, the Hebrew kindly lends us far more insight! For instance, these same letters give us: נאם, ne'um and אמן, aman, the former indicating an utterance or oracle that is about to be released, while the latter, in its verbal form is a word that means to be firm, to build up, to support or nurture and to establish. It conveys a faithfulness and trustworthiness that one surely could depend on!

Thus, YHVH seems to be conveying that the terribleness or intensity of the Plagues is about to increase at His declaration, His Oracle – Pharaoh could depend on that! What oracle you ask? LET MY PEOPLE GO! This phrase has a gematria of 859, the same as the phrase "Lost in Oz". We may have jumped off the deep end there, but, again, if you haven't seen the old movie 'The Wizard of Oz' in quite some time, then you would, by all means, be greatly served to go back and revisit it in light of what you've learned thus far! The Powers That Be use the magic of 'twisted words' in all forms of media to show how omnipotent they are by telling you, to your face what their plans are, and laughing all the while the masses wallow in the squalor of ignorance!

What is more, there's a wild connection that can be seen in Leviticus 11:15, which is found on the surface seemingly discussing unclean fowls, yet the specific bird mentioned in the English text is that of the Raven, the Hebrew has it: H#6158, ערב, 'oreb, which is etymologically (Not coincidentally) related to the 8th plague – locusts – Arbeh:

The sentence in Leviticus reads: Every raven after his kind: את כל-ערב למינו - ET Chol -'oreb lemiynu. The word miyn seen translated as 'kind' could also indicate 'numbered'. Thus, every raven/arov shall be numbered…could this be hinting at the great swarms of the 8th plague of locusts an horrific and future gruesome event shown depicted in the text of Revelation 9 wherein these same locusts are portrayed as demonic chimera vomited from the bowels of Sheol?

Furthermore, those same letters seen in 'refuse' style: H#4484, מנא, mene, as seen in Daniel 5:25,26. ...*Mene, Mene Tekel Upharsin*...YHVH has numbered your kingdom and finished it. You are weighed in the balances and are found wanting. Your Kingdom is divided and given to the Medes and Persians! Though we're speaking of Pharaoh here, the Greater Exodus Plagues will see the dynastic kingdom of the Anti-Messiah – Babylon, who is supported by the Elite, also weighed in the balance and destroyed!

These future plagues are going to restructure the worlds Powers thus causing the Proud and Haughty to fall! This is emphasized in:

> 2Samuel 1:19: *The beauty of Israel is slain upon thy high places: how are the mighty fallen!*

It is this author's opinion, that out of these amalgamated 'Powers', in keeping with Daniel's prophecy, that you can shortly expect to see a League of Nations gathered to form another Medo-Persian Empire. These will be gathered out of such nations as: Afghanistan, Pakistan, Turkmenistan, Georgia, Turkey, Iraq, and Saudi Arabia, all assembled together probably in alliance with China.

If this ominous declaration precedes the 8th plague, then the final stages of the collapse of the Egyptian-Pharonic Empire and the future extermination of the Anti-Messiah's kingdom hinge on this 8th - plague of Locusts! What? These little winged fliers? Shall we see?

David Mathews

The Locusts Are Coming

Traditional narrative and the perspective of our forebears who saw through a 'glass darkly' have colored our current End-Times paradigm. What if we could look through the clear lens of the Hebrew Language and aided by the Ruach, see a much more precise image? I firmly believe we now can! I must warn you though, dear Reader, the protective bubble that most Christians live in called the Rapture is exploding as we speak! These things are already in motion and the 'Rapturists' - they're still here! Now, considering that...

Straightaway, before preceding with our look at these 'locusts', I'd like to call attention to the following verse and perhaps another hidden insight that will enable our understanding:

> Exodus 10:4 *Else, if thou refuse to let my people go, behold, tomorrow will I bring the locusts into thy coast:*

See the word 'coast'? H#1366, גבול, ghevul, translated as boundary, border or space? It is from the root indicating a twisted cord or rope, as a line used to measure rods for boundaries. Likewise, this reminds us of a DNA helix and things get extremely mystical here requiring unconventional thinking! Moreover, we find it somewhat reminiscent of the Scarlet Rope of Rahab (The Book of Joshua) used to help the spies escape. This is a word which came from the same root Bel-Lamed, but with the Chet appended חבל – forming Hebel – a powerful word which can indicate to destroy economically or financially. It is also a word associated with the pledge or collateral for the guarantee of a loan.

Having shared that with you, dear Reader, let me advise you: The current Pharaoh's World banking system is about to be spoiled: Their loans, notes, collateral, bonds, fiat currency and all their other 'holdings' destroyed and what's left, handed over

The Exodus Keys

to the DEPARTING REMNANT who will be EXITING EGYPT – BABYLON! By the way, this has nothing to do with the prosperity message of the Church, who contrarily, will find themselves destitute because of having placed their trust in the same World's system! Surely you remember the great line from the 1992 presidential campaign? It's the Economy Stupid! As we speak, those involved in Politics, economics, government, etc. are all bedfellows with the Elite who control the purse strings of the world's Banking system!

Interestingly, in hindsight, Rahab is later told to let the same rope down again, but this time the wording is changed to describe a scarlet rope – a tiqvah – תקוה, this scarlet rope will ensure the salvation of she and her family! This reminds us of the Blood – the Twisted cord or rope of the DNA helix – of Messiah affixed to the doors of Israel during the final 10th Exodus plague!

**Remember Egypt's coast is separated from Goshen during these plagues. Here, we must ask ourselves, what prohibited the plagues from entering Goshen, since no physical barrier existed? Could there be more to this just discussed, 'boundary of Blood'? Let me call your attention to Exodus 8:22 where YHVH declares: *And I will sever in that day the land of Goshen...*Understanding what happened to cause this distinction is paramount to understanding the salvation and subsequent preservation of Israel during the Exodus plagues and how the coming Greater Exodus Plagues will affect latter-day Israel – you and I!

והפליתי ביום ההוא את-ארץ גשן, V'hiphleyiti B'yowm h'huw ET-Eretz Goshen... *And I will sever in that day the land of Goshen...*

The word for sever is H#6395, פלה, palah, and does mean to 'sever', set apart, but also hints at something wonderfully and amazingly constructed! Now, pay attention to the word h'huw, which indicates a masculine pronoun followed by the Alef-Tav-

Eretz! In other words, h'huw – The He – The Him, the One Who is the Alef-Tav – Eretz – The Land. The HE – The Him, The Alef-Tav will set apart, sever, by constructing something wonderful and amazing between Goshen and Egypt!

How Could This Be?
What Are We Not 'Seeing'?

Hold That Thought and
Look at Goshen for A Bit…

If you recall in our 1st part of this series we established that Goshen would not have been in Egypt proper, rather it would have been located outside the border of Mitsrayim-Egypt. Based on this premise, it is my opinion the Goshen would have been the location of Eden Proper!

For emphasis of my point, let me share an extra-biblical excerpt from the book of Jubilees.

**Take note: *And he (Shem) knew that the Garden of Eden is the Holy of Hollies, and the dwelling place of YHVH, and Mount Sinai, the center of the desert, and Mount Zion, the center of the navel of the earth, these three, opposite one another, were created as sanctuaries.* [Jubilees 8:17 R.H. Charles, D.Litt. D.D 1917][#18]

Based on that criteria, Goshen was undoubtedly a SANCTUARY as well, and as such, then it should fit into one of the 3-areas above! What in reality is a Sanctuary, truly? From H#4720, the Hebrew definition has it: מקדש, miqdash, a set apart, consecrated place. This word 'miqdash' hides an intriguing secret. As we break the word apart, we have the Mem indicating a womb, a

---

[#18] *The Book OF JUBILEES*, 1895. Translated from the Ethiopic Text by R.H. Charles, D.Litt. D.D. Public Domain.

place of origin, the birthing place. In Hebrew grammar, there are 2 forms of the Mem, מ, open; and ם, closed.

The Sages teach that the Mem represents Torah – both the revealed word - מ an open Mem and the hidden or secret word – ם, the closed Mem. The letter Mem represents the Waters of Creation, revealed both in the physical woman's womb and in its place in the expanse of heavens – שמים, shamayim, first seen in Genesis 1 where it incubates the SEED of Creation – who would later become The WORD OF ELOHIYM MADE FLESH – YAHSHUA our Messiah! This is confirmed in the text of:

> 2Peter 3:5 ...*by the Word of YHVH the earth was formed out of water and by water.*

The remaining letters of miqdash: Qof-Dalet-Shin, can be arranged to form שקד, Shaqad, which relates to the Almond shaped cups of the menorah that contained the Oil for the Light. However, it also indicates to be sleepless, to guard or watch over.

Thus, a miqdash, or sanctuary is a place where the Living Water, who, like the Menorah inside the womb of the Tabernacle, form an embryonic sac encompassing with light, what or whomever is inside, watching over, guarding, enveloping the SEED within! **This is your Goshen! Your protected Sanctuary!** Look at what King David, the Psalmist had to say:

> Psalms 121:4 *Indeed, He who watches over Israel will neither slumber nor sleep!*

In summation, Mem is also a guide, a caregiver, an instructor and the one who gives direction. Mem takes on the mystical FORM of the Genesis 1:27 ADAM – having both the characteristics of Man and Woman! Thus, as a sanctuary it releases seed as it procreates whilst it also wombs that seed, protecting and nourishing until the time for the Delivery!

I know this was a long diversion, so, how about our returning to look at Goshen?

As we continue our Goshen detective work, upon heading toward Egypt Jacob sends Judah beforehand to his Joseph who is already Viceroy in the land: Judah's purpose? - *"To direct his (Jacob's) face unto Goshen"* - להורת לפניו גשנה, lehoroyte lepahnayiv goshnah: Here we take our insinuated definitions out of the Hebrew word pictures and show you what the KJV English cannot! For instance:

The word or more literally, the Hebraic phrase for direct - lehoroyte – comes from the root Yarah, *to teach, or to flow as water* – to go before his face – unto Goshnah. Goshnah has a numeric value of 358, the same as Mashiach! This could read: *Jacob sends Judah ahead To Joseph to get HIM - To teach the flowing/Living water of Torah before his face until Messiah comes!*

Ironically, today's Sages teach that Judah would latter establish Torah schools in Egypt, yet, in my opinion, this isn't consistent with Scripture as Joseph was the one being taught in the Schools of Torah! This biased mindset still exists and is a major detriment to the reconciliation of the 2 Houses! To be candid with you, it is the Torah of Joseph – not Judah – that formed the Body of Messiah; epitomizing that same Mashiach Ben Joseph whom Judah wasn't expecting when Yahshua first came and the very same personification previously found in their brother Joseph who's Egyptian countenance first caused them to fail to recognize him when they initially went down into Egypt to purchase grain. It was the legacy of this Joseph whom the Exodus Pharaoh did not know! That being said: How exactly was Goshen 'severed' from Egypt?

Without doubt, it is plausible to consider Goshen as a part of Eden proper the original 'Sanctuary' for the DNA of the Creator, as well as, a gateway or portal where HE – the Memra – or

Manifest Presence - He who was the embodiment of YHVH that would descend by times through this gateway upon the earth! If my thesis be so, perhaps He – who was also personified in The Flaming Sword – bound on either side by Cherubim and later depicted in the example of the Ark of The Covenant, or Mercy Seat – would also be expected to appear here to welcome the Son(s) of YHVH – Israel (who functioned as the 2nd Adam) to Goshen or 'back to Eden'! Genesis 3:24: **Let's look!**

...Flaming Sword, which turned every way flaming... flaming in Hebrew is H#3858, להט, lahat, though translated as 'flaming', it also indicates the mystical ability to hide something secretly. Curiously, it has the same gematria – 44 – as dam, the Hebrew word for blood, and yalad, to bring forth a son, as well as, Teleh, a lamb!

The Power of the Blood and how it was hidden remained a true mystery until the coming of Messiah! Blood speaks! In fact, it is known that blood absorbs light, which gives credence to an innovative science called photo-acoustics, a means by which one shoots a laser light across a blood cell causing it to release stored sound, and reveal specific blood types along with a host of other cellular DNA encrypted messages!

Furthermore, if we look at the Hebrew word Dam, written דם yet read it in reverse from left to right we get: מד, Mad, a word indicating a garment and to apportion or measure out something! In keeping with that, to 'put on' Messiah means to clothe yourself in His Blood which speaks of True deliverance! Because that blood was never tainted with sin! Indeed, this blood cries out revealing who your Father is! In our near future, the ability to determine who are the Sons of Elohiym will take on a new meaning as the Light of His Word courses through the Veins of the Remnant! This blood will cry out in testimony to the Paternity Claim of Sonship necessary to inherit the Land! HalleluYah!

Back to the Flaming Sword Connection Above...

The word Sword, H#2719, חרב, chereb, is defined as a cutting instrument, but also, something signifying an edge or BORDER. It also hints at: That which is waste, desolate (Tohu V'bohu – the earth was without form and void) without water, decaying, and dried up. These same letters style: Bet-Chet-Resh, giving us 'Bechor' designating the firstborn and Chet-Bet-Resh, chavar, to stripe or wound! The living translations tell us that YHVH was perhaps hinting at the FIRSTBORN who would be striped, wounded in order to restore the waste and desolate Place – i.e. Eden and its Adam? After the fall Adam became Tohu V' Bohu! Only to be reinvigorated once Yahshua took the stripes or plagues upon His Body on the Execution Stake on behalf of them!

The phrase *'which turned every way'* is written: המתהפכת, h'mithapeket, the root of which is: הפך, haphak, defined as to turn, overthrow, overturn, to transform and to turn again or away. It indicates 'to reverse', or carry away!

Could this sentence indicate that the FIERY BLOOD MAN – WHOSE DNA – MANIFESTED IN MESSIAH - WOULD TRANSFORM THE BORDER OF EDEN – GOSHEN functioning like the Sword of Eden in TURNING AWAY ANY WHO WOULD APPROACH in an untoward manner? Perhaps bring a plague upon them? This does indeed seem the purpose of the Fiery Sword at Eden and fits the blueprint for Goshen as well! There is a dual role being depicted depending on the relationship with this Sword!

For instance, while turning away the enemies of YHVH at Eden, concurrently, for those inside the Sanctuary, this Fiery Blood Man, this Sword Man - would also be seen facing Israel-Goshen while turning His Back to the PLAGUES, thus taking them upon Himself, those very plagues which were intended to lay waste, make Tohu V'bohu, or cause to decay, the children of Israel now returning to Eden/Goshen.

In addition, as He takes the Plagues upon His Body He would stand at the BORDER – THE VEIL and thus, reverse their curses, overturning or carrying them away! He would literally 'TAKE ON HIMSELF THE PLAGUES' – in the manner of His Crucifixion being STRIPED OR WOUNDED while protecting those within the Sanctuary of His Blood who would be born again!

This is the Goshen EFFECT! This is exactly what the Prophet Isaiah speaks of in Isaiah 53, and sadly, to the dishonor of our Jewish brothers, they don't even want to discuss this chapter and if you find one who will, he speaks as if it is a reference to Israel as a whole!

**See Isaiah 53:3,4,5 *He is despised and rejected of men; a man of sorrows, and acquainted with grief: and we hid as it were our faces from him; he was despised, and we esteemed him not. Surely he hath borne our griefs, and carried our sorrows: yet we did esteem him stricken, smitten of God, and afflicted. But he was wounded for our transgressions, he was bruised for our iniquities: the chastisement of our peace was upon him; and with his stripes we are healed.*

Likewise, we see this epitomized in the 10th plague where the Blood is once again applied to the Doorway – the entrance to EDEN-GOSHEN. While Messiah stands at the threshold of Israel's house, the Death Angel comes. At this threshold, the ALTAR of every home, we find Messiah turning His back to absorb the stripes, H#2250, חבורה, chabbura, stripes, from chavar, to unite, or bind together! Perhaps we can more fully understand Paul speaking of "The Fellowship or union of His sufferings…"

Incidentally, this word chavar has the same root letters as Sword – Chereb!

Later, on Golgotha's hill, Yahshua does exactly the same thing! Turning His back to the lictors and absorbing the STRIPES – PLAGUES that were ours, thereby establishing a Boundary of Blood the crossing of which, would cause us to be Born Again!

We see the same pattern of blood boundaries throughout the Tanak (Old Testament) such as when David fights Goliath. For perspective, Israel was in the valley of Elah, H#425, אלה, rendered 'an oak' or Terebinth Tree. This is literally a picture of the Long-Lived Tree planted by those participants at a covenant cutting! The execution stake at Golgotha was a 'long-lived' tree!

The place in this valley of Elah was between Shochoh (In Hebrew H#7755, שוכה, from a root indicating to shut in for protection and restraint) and Azekah, H#5825, עזקה, to dig about or fence in! The place or valley between these two was also called Ephesdammim, H#658, אפס דמים, translated as 'The Border or Boundary of Blood!' Ephes is from the root Pas – as in the coat of many colors, and Pesach – Passover – an interesting phrase that indicates a strong hand, which covers!

This is physically the place between the Boundaries, the place Where the Hand of YHVH would 'pass over' or cover those inside with the garment called the Kethoneth Passim – also known as the Coat of Many colors, but which would originally have been The Blood – Garment of Light – Colors worn by Adam and Eve (Chavah) prior to the fall!

Hopefully, by now you are beginning to understand the significance of finding your Goshen? Now, prayerfully, we can appreciate even more the consequence of being out of Egypt or Babylon when these future plagues come! And they are coming!

Chapter 8

The 8ᵗʰ Plague: Locusts

How apropos that this is the 8ᵗʰ plague, 8 being the number associated with the letter Chet, the fenced off place, the DNA helix, and the locale where new beginnings occur! As such, this plague was a particularly ferocious event coming on the heels of the previous assault on Egypt's animals and barley crops, which had left them already sorely decimated. The remaining Wheat crop is just now greening and these supposed vermin are set to destroy what's left! Let's look closer…

First, before going too far, I want to skip ahead a tad to Exodus 10:7 where Pharaoh's servants make an astonishing statement: *'knowest thou not yet, that Egypt is destroyed?'*

הטרם תדע כי אבדה מצרים, h'terem tedah ki 'avdah Mitsrayim… The word destroyed – 'avdah, H#6, אבדה, indicates to destroy, exterminate, and to utterly fail. Again, pay close attention to the Hebrew word for Egypt – Mitsrayim that is defined below!

- Mitsrayim, H#4714   מצרים

    It is usually translated as 'between 2 straights'. Yet, I want to zero in here for a second. All Hebrew linguists agree that the name Mitsrayim is not Semitic.

Interestingly, some attribute its root to a related word metzar, meaning – a BOUNDARY OR BORDER.

I must state however, that in fact, most agree that the ancient origin for the name of Egypt or Mitsrayim, actually comes from the Son of Ham, H#2526, חם, Cham, and is rendered: Khemet, literally 'the Black land' for its rich soil.

This is quite interesting in our study, as the **Land of Khemet-Egypt** – is said to be the root of the ancient Science of Alchemy (Klein gives us alchemy) n. medieval chemistry – old French alquemie (13th century), alchimie (14th cent.) (French alchimie) from Latin alchemia, from Arabic al-kimiya, a compound of al - 'the', and Greek, chimeia, chimia, 'the art of the black land (Egypt)', again from Greek Chimia, 'Black-land, Egypt', from Egyptian khem, khame, 'black'. The derivation from Greek chymeia, 'pouring', from the stem of cheein, 'to pour', is folk etymology.[#19]

Alchemy, as a science, was the ancient quest for the secret and mystical arts of Transmutation: both of metals and humans – you'll note the etymological connection to Chimera – the hybridization of two or more species. Curiously, we get the English word 'chemistry' from alchemy. Oh, by the way, today's Elite, the Freemasons, Illuminists, etc. are all consumed with alchemy! Incidentally, such transmutation can occur on multiply levels: In particular those that are Spiritual, Physical, or Mental as the 'host' has its DNA manipulated through various methods.

These methods include, but are not limited to: EMF frequencies, the insertion of corrupted DNA into the host (Vaccinations, food sources, etc.) Sexual deviancy, and other surgical alterations! Incidentally, in keeping with their quest for transmutable supremacy, for the first time in United States history an openly

---

[#19] See W. Muss-Arnolt, Transactions of the *American Philological Association*, vol XXIII p. 149. Public Domain.

transgender Man/Woman has been nominated for federal office – Sec. of Health…

What Does This Have to Do With This Plague?

Candidly, Boundaries could imply far more than just a Land marker! It could encompass efforts to cross over these boundaries of the Spiritual, Physical, Mental, Sexual and other realms! In addition, if we look at the numeric values, Mitsrayim's value is 380, the same as 'Lashon' – the word meaning tongue or language. In addition, 380 is also the value of H#7549, רקיע, raqiya`, rendered 'firmament' – that which is stretched out – an overlayment, to press out - as in the expanse of heaven separating the waters above from the waters below.

In that context, the Tongue becomes a Raqiya, a firmament or boundary between the Heavens, controlling what is allowed to pass through! He who controls the tongue controls the boundaries of his own body! Let that sink in for a moment!

In the same fashion, the Raqiya – the firmament or waters above the waters, becomes the boundary, or border; in reality, the instrument tasked with filtering or disseminating words or light and its power to all those inside the Sanctuary, whether the earth or the Wilderness Tabernacle or the Boundary – Raqiya of Goshen! All the while, protecting them as well! To continue, 380 is also the value of השמלה, h'simlah, a phrase meaning 'The Garment'!

This reminds us of the Body of Flesh created or pressed out for Messiah. Ironically, the Resh-Qof root of raqiya hints at that which decays or putrefies!

Yahshua came in a decaying, fleshly body in the image of the first Adam, having taken upon Himself the Plagues of Death and Destruction, that He might restore Light – Life to those within the Raqiya or Expanse, the Covering Garment known as "His Body".

If we add the 2nd word in our verse above from page 82 - Avadah, to destroy, it seems something sinister is going on behind the scenes between the Magicians of Pharaoh and his efforts at controlling the People. Further, what if, that 'Lashon or tongue' which plainly hints at their efforts to communicate, has been destroyed? This seems contradictory though, since the magicians are still talking to Pharaoh at this point aren't they? What then, is really taking place here? Let's ask a few questions:

So, if they're talking amongst themselves then, exactly with what or with who have they lost communication? What if their magical efforts that are, in all honesty, rooted in Alchemy – The creating of Transmuted Species, were suddenly turned against them? I find this laughable as I write, simply because they're already preparing to introduce to the 'World – WHIRLED' – those spinning in Dorothy's tornado – an alien **benevolent** transmuted species who will be presented as the gods able to solve the Earth's problems!

Moreover, suppose today's 5G & 6G technology along with the HARP and other EMF that allow the Elite to communicate subliminally and effectuate DNA manipulation among the population is suddenly cut off or turned against them, like the predicament the Magicians found themselves in?

Moreover, what of the Original Transmuted or Hybridized clones and their progenitors, the Fallen Ones themselves? Is it possible that this plague involves a mutiny or rebellion of sorts within the ranks of those Hordes – Swarms - Locusts of Hell (Revelation 9:3-11).

A Plague, wherein Egypt-Babylon and their Elite Controllers become the prey rather than the predator?

The Exodus Keys

**Remember the SONS OF ELOHIYM have been sealed at this time! They're in Goshen! Tread carefully, dear Reader and as yourself: Is this something conjured out of a Science Fiction or Conspiracist Mindset or Have We Looked Behind the Curtain? Click your red shoes together and see if you wind up in Kansas! Furthermore, look at the following pictograph of 4 of the pantheon of Egyptian gods!

If this seems improbable, remember all these presented below are HYBRID GODS of Egypt! Ra, Horus, Sobek, Seth![20]

Could these Locusts be pointing toward those Crossed Boundaries?

At this point, things may get a bit convoluted. Was this a new Plague or a return (Much Worse This Time) of a previous one? The word used here for Locusts is H#697, ארבה, 'arbeh, and is translated inoffensively as 'locusts', but originates from the root rabah, רבה, to become great, numerous, to be multiplied and is the same as the word used to describe the Swarms of Flies we saw while discussing the 4th – 'arbeh, plague.

---

[20] Images by Jeff Dahl (talk contribs). Used with permission.
https://en.wikipedia.org/wiki/User:Jeff_Dahl?rdfrom=commons:User:Jeff_Dahl

**Note: This is the 8th – a doubling of 4 – meaning to do again.

The number 4 – arbeh is found written with a single letter, the Dalet which represents a doorway, while 8 – Shemoneh, H#8083, שמנה – the Chet, indicating a fence or ladder is pointing toward a DNA helix. Those same letters can be arranged to form משנה, Mishnah, which also means to 'double', to copy, a repetition, next in rank or hierarchy! 8 is a doubling, do over, a repeat, an increase of – 4! If read from right to left the above root rabah becomes, 'Habar': Meaning an astrologer, one who worships the stars. Specifically, the gods of those stars! Could the Prophet Isaiah have looked into the future, our day and revealed this exact scenario now taking place in our lives?

Note Isaiah 47:5,12,13 *Sit thou silent (No tongue-communication) and get thee into darkness* **(the 9th plague?) *O daughter of the Chaldeans* **(Babylon the Mother of Harlots)***: for thou shalt no more be called,* **The Lady of Kingdoms**. *Stand now with thine enchantments, and with the multitude of thy sorceries, wherein thou hast labored from thy youth; if so be thou shalt be able to profit, if so be thou mayest prevail.*

Thou art wearied in the multitude of thy counsels. Let now the astrologers **(HABAR)** *the stargazers, the monthly prognosticators, stand up, and save thee from these things that shall come upon thee.* Seems the ancient prophet is indulging in a bit of sarcasm!

**Note 'The Lady' above, from the Hebrew H#1404, גברת, gebereth, translated here as a mistress, is also from the same root as Gibbowr – the Mighty Ones, those who act insolently toward YHVH! Egypt and Babylon became the MISTRESS TO THESE FALLEN ONES! There is no doubt that the Elite of our day are themselves prostituted to the same!

Do you think it's coincidental that these 'Locusts' – ארבה – are etymologically the same as the infamous giant called Arba -

ארבע, the father of Anak and referred to as the greatest of the giants (Anakim)? No? Look at the root רבע, raba`, to lie stretched out, to lie down, the copulation of a woman with a beast, cattle breeding. These BEASTS are not going to be satisfied with the plans of the Elite, neither that of the Anti-Messiah! They are the ones controlling and will not submit to the mortal Elites!

The Hiphil tense of raba indicates to cause or to suffer to gender, to misuse that which YHVH intended to be propagated as in a man with woman, male with female. The word is found in Leviticus 18 and 19. In a sobering litany, here we find the universal progression of sexual debauchery: Incest, Adultery, Homosexuality/Lesbianism, and bestiality! These are the 4- MAJOR AREAS OF PERVERSION SEEN IN AMERIKA [Sic] TODAY! There are also subgroups; of which, pedophilia fits into the 3rd category! In addition, arba - ארבע, indicates the number 4 – Dalet – a door or entrance.

Consequently, I found it interesting that Revelation 9 speaks of four angels being loosed – the Greek doesn't reveal much here – yet, the Hebrew does: 4, ARBA – Malachim – 4 angels - from the Euphrates, which comes from the Hebrew H#6578, פרת, Perath, meaning to burst forth, to become fruitful. Please remember, the Euphrates River flows through the PERSIAN EMPIRE! Is this telling us that 4 Messengers of Arba that original Giant, the greatest of the Nephylim – is being set loose? Skeptical still? Then ask yourself what in the heck was Jude speaking of in the following text!

> Jude 1:5,6 *I will therefore put you in remembrance, though you once knew this how that YHVH having saved the people out of the land of Egypt, afterward destroyed them that believed not. And the angels, which kept not their first estate, but left their own habitation, He hath reserved in everlasting chains under darkness unto the judgment of the great day!*

The Greek text actually says He has reserved them, meaning to attend to carefully, for the judgment of the great day – What day? The Great and Terrible Day of YHVH! This is not talking about their judgment, rather that they will be part of Man's judgment!

This is consistent with the scenario known as the 'DAYS OF NOAH' about which Yahshua makes reference to in Matthew 24:37. The Hebrew text of Genesis reveals that during Noah's day the floodgates of heaven and those in the bowels of the earth were opened. It is my opinion that the Flood out of the Mouth of the Dragon of Revelation 12 will coincide with this 8th plague! At such time, here we will see the Fallen Ones cast down to the earth and those held in chains under the earth released to torment men! Though the Sons of Elohiym will be in Goshen!

Stand Fast My Brothers! Make your Calling and Election Sure! Seek the Face of Elohiym; listen to and for His Voice. Walk humbly before Him in Righteousness. Turn not to the right or left. Do not be dismayed at the signs in the heavens, neither swayed at the devices of man. For YHVH will not be mocked. While they cower in fear waiting for the mountains to fall on them, you will be put into the Cleft of the Rock until the times of Refreshing that is to come!

It may seem as if I'm employing shock tactics in order to drive home my point. Fear mongering some might accuse. However, what I've provided you dear Reader is a renewed look at End-Times prophecy through the lens of the only mechanism provided us that is without reproof – the Hebrew language of the Scriptures.

With that being said, there is no doubt that many, if not all, the Theologians of the past miss-interpreted the same. Some, out of their religious bias formed a prejudiced opinion that has been culpable in the masses being unprepared for the devastation of these plagues and the ensuing apostate condition which will flourish in the aftermath leaving many with a mindset that is often referred to as 'The Great Falling Away'

If our efforts succeed in awakening those currently sleeping and foster a renewed interest in the Truth, then our tireless exertions will have been rewarded exponentially! Now, if you will, prepare yourself for the next in this series of the horrific plagues! You will never look at the book of Exodus the same again! So, once more: Unleash the hounds!

Chapter 9

The 9th Plague: Darkness[21]

Exodus 10:21-23

After our in-depth look at the previous plagues and YHVH's promise to intensify each one, from the natural, this 9th plague of Darkness seems the least severe and almost a contradiction of that promised intensification. However, YHVH said differently, although, it doesn't seem to affect Egypt in a physically

---

[21] Sabine Alex http://www.torah-illustrations.blogspot.com/
Used with permission.

threatening manner like the others. Yet, out of all the others, it seems to mirror the current situation of the 2020/21 CoViD-19 plan-demic. What do I mean?

Simply, to put this 9th plague in perspective, we'll look at some unorthodox connections that will help to peel back the layers enabling us to understand what this dreadful ancient plague and its future appearance really consists of. For example: The ignoble Covid-19 scourge was a long-term part of a greater plan of the Elite for the seduction and enslaving of the Masses. Observe:

The 1st Interesting Connection

CoViD-19 has the same consonantal letters in Hebrew as כבוד, Kavod - translated as glory, weighty, heavy, and burdensome. Curiously, the total values: Of Kavod whose gematria is 32 + the 19 give us 51. This number 51 is also the gematria of H#3608, כלא, kala, meaning to close, hinder, to restrain, to hold back something, to finish, complete, to imprison or to confine! Kala is cognate with the word for Bride – kallah. This pandemic is an attempt to imprison the Bride of Messiah!

Everything being done regarding this man-made scourge is doing just that! Working to imprison the masses by restraining free thought and our individual God-given rights. Ironically, fear and lazy ignorance and acquiescence are their best tools!

Therefore, it is not a stretch to liken this to the beginnings of what is surely, a plague of Darkness! In like manner to CoViD, this 9th plague depicted in Exodus affects the social status and intimacy of all Egypt, replacing it with a heaviness that brought their destruction to completion and exacerbated their imprisonment!

In passing, did you notice that there are 51 Hebrew letters in the following verse of our Hebrew text? Coincidence? I think not! *And YHVH said unto Moses, Stretch out thine hand toward heaven, that there may be darkness over the land of Egypt, even darkness which may be felt.*

Let's get back to our accustomed habit of dissecting these texts from a purely Hebraic perspective. By doing so we take what is to some an inscrutable, archaic tongue – Hebrew – and, while knowing that according to Zephaniah 3:8,9 it is being restored as the pure language of the People – we take to this language, that is the encapsulated Mind of the Creator as our source to tell us what He is saying rather than relying on the hit-or-miss interpretations of fallible men! So, please…

Observe: The darkness is described as: *'over'* the land of Egypt – על-ארץ מצרים, Al-'erets Mitsrayim. The preposition 'על' can mean upon, over, against, as well as, a yoke of servitude. Could this indicate that Darkness, as an ominous presence – perhaps a literal Divine Entity - sets himself upon or against Egypt tightening the Yoke upon its neck? The gematria of 'Al-'erets' is 391; the same as the Hebrew name for Joshua, H#3091, יהושע, Yahoshua, which is a compound of YHVH and yashah, a word that can mean, to save, deliverance from dangers and distresses, and to preserve, but, also (Take Note) to take **private vengeance**!

With this in mind, rather than receive the Vengeance of YHVH, Egypt could have taken the Torah - The Yoke of Messiah - upon themselves as described in:

> Matthew 11:28-30 *Come to me, all you who labor and are heavy laden, and I will give you rest. Take my yoke upon you, and learn from me, for I am gentle and lowly in heart: and you will find rest for your souls. For my yoke is easy, and my burden is light.*

Instead, Egypt placed a yoke upon the necks of Israel with the same burdensome laws of their pantheon of gods, the head of which, or supreme deity, Pharaoh symbolized. Yahshua would later call attention to the Yoke of Torah that should have been easy, yet the Pharisees of His day made it burdensome! The same can be said for the innumerable 'statutes and codes' enacted against the People today to further enslave them. Let's take a short aside... Sorta like the old childhood game: Let's kick the can down the road a bit! ☺

Why Pick on the Pharisees?

The Pharisees were condemned by Yahshua for always seeking a sign, you might say, the same as Pharaoh, who always needed a sign in order to be convinced of the validity of Moshe's office! Further, the root of Pharisee comes from that of Pharaoh and many, including Josephus hint that the origin of this sect came from those exiled in Egypt because of having been persecuted by the family of the Maccabees. These 'Pharisees' after the order of Pharaoh built a temple in Leontopolis, Egypt, adapting many of the burdensome pagan rites and rituals and man-made laws similar to the rabbinic laws today that are contrary to Torah!

Back to Darkness: The Mystery of Creation

It is imperative to comprehend this 9th plague called 'Darkness'; else our understanding of the initial Exodus plague and the one looming before us during the Great Tribulation will not be enhanced. To our vexation, the KJV English text only shares 3-verses regarding this plague, an act leaving much room for supposition, speculation, etc. Hence, the reason that most of today's eschatology experts will be found wrong in their positions regarding this event, one that left an indelible label stamped forever upon Egypt and that will surely do so again, upon those in our future who endure it!

So, Let's Dig Deeper Shall We?

The Hebrew word for darkness is fascinating - written: H#2822, חשך, choshek, and rendered darkness, obscurity, a secret place, and to hide or conceal. Figuratively, it means misery, destruction, death, ignorance, sorrow and wickedness. It is my opinion that the translators misunderstood Choshek and thus, expressed it negatively. Buckle up dear Reader! This is going to get bumpy!

For instance, the same letters of Choshek when rearranged and written Shin-Kaf-Chet give us: to forget, to be lost to memory, to find or discover, to come up. Did this Darkness conceal or hide - literally 'to cover' Egypt and cause them to be lost to memory? If so, whose memory? YHVH alone has the power to 'remember no more'!

What happens when He 'remembers you no more'? Your posterity is cut off, leading to the 10th plague, death of the 1st-born!

So what exactly is this darkness? Have we also misunderstood Choshek? As I mentioned, there's nothing much to help in our text of only 3 verses, even so, Choshek/Darkness has to be significant as it was first mentioned in Genesis 1:2. Furthermore, here in the Creation Account of Genesis 1 the darkness - like here in Exodus - is also said to be upon – Al – the Face of the Deep, as compared to 'upon the erets/land of Egypt' during this 9th plague – while simultaneously the Ruach moved upon the Face of the Waters.

**Observe: The Ruach or Spirit moved upon 2 distinct places: Deep and Waters.

Perhaps here we have a clue regarding the Plague of Darkness? Deep is the Hebrew word H#8415, תהום, tehowm, defined as 'deep, depths, deep places and the abyss or grave, as in the sea and its subterranean vaults. The root, *huwm*, indicates an uproar or tumultuous agitation, a great noise of disturbance!

To put this in perspective, after Genesis 1:1 it is undeniable that a major catastrophic event took place causing the Perfection of Creation to become Tohu V'bohu. Genesis 1:2 Reveals that who or whatever causing such an agitation was relegated to this 'DEEP' – tehowm, and did not go peacefully, rather there's a great furor stirring in its depths! Based on our Hebrew definitions, *it appears the Entity Darkness is called upon to enforce the bondage or servitude and stands over, or against whatever is imprisoned in the Deep!* Similar to what a jailer would do at a prison.

The word for deep - Tehowm is seen 80 times in the Tanak. Across the Scriptures, the numeral 80 symbolizes the start or duration of freedom from oppressors. Moshe was 80-years old at the time of the Exodus. It is connected to the Hebrew letter Pey indicating the Mouth or speech! In Hebrew letters and numbers are interchangeable. Each letter being a number by itself. For instance, Alef = 1, Bet = 2, Gimmel = 3 and so forth. The number 80 is written with the Pey which is styled when written Pey – Hey, פה. This is noteworthy because of the word pictures of each letter/number which, in this case points out that 'Hey - Breath' and Life – Seed – Word' are birthed out of the Mouth, thus death and life are in its power!

Here in Genesis and in our Exodus text, it seems Darkness as a restraining force, is an entity or a Being who stands in opposition to or as protection against, those restrained in the Deep and after that the gods are found ruling Egypt where He-Darkness functions as the executor of judgment or Freedom for Israel!

As we continue, from Genesis 1:2 we see that the 'original' darkness/choshek existed *before* YHVH says, "Let there be Light". After this declaration and subsequent to Choshek a 2nd 'darkness' is revealed as separated from (Perhaps revealed by) that 1st Primordial Light and thereupon called 'Night', H#3915, לילה, or in Hebrew, lailah, much like the distinction between the first LIGHT-'Owr and the 2nd Light – Ma'owr - of Genesis 1:14.

When we study the Hebrew language it is imperative to remember that no word is used as filler material, neither frivolously. In every instance, a hidden message is being conveyed that takes the Student deeper into the mysteries of its depths. In addition, the individual letters that comprise that same word will retain their original individual word pictures. When found in another word that new word will add another definition and dimension, yet their intrinsic value remains. Allow me to show you a quick example as we segue into the next chapter. Hold your place here and we'll return to connect all these dots!

Chapter 10

Lailah and Heylel

We were just looking at one of the words for darkness or night rendered as: Lailah.

Did you notice that these same letters of lailah לילה give us H#1966, הילל, heylel, often translated as (Lucifer) as in 'light-bearer', brightness, to shine and is related to ילל, yalal, yelel, to howl or lament in anguish or mourning?

Is it possible that the original Darkness – Choshek – served as a garment for both Choshek and Lailah who were ECHAD – One - United at one time, yet, because of the events between Genesis 1:1 and 1:2 (Some call this the 'Gap Theory') they had to be separated and that Lailah now represents this Heylel – Lucifer, the Fallen One who is cast down from his place in the Choshek, to a lower place in the bowels – tehowm of the earth where he becomes Satan – the adversary? In which case, you're probably asking how could Darkness be a considered a garment? Have a look…

It appears this separation could have been what Yahshua referenced when He remarks in Luke 10:18: *I beheld Satan as lightning fall from heaven*. Why did he fall or was he cast down? Isaiah 14 and Ezekiel 28 give insight, but we don't have time to address it thoroughly here. Suffice it to say that in Ezekiel 28:16

YHVH says He will *'cast him as profane out of the mountain'*...this gives us a clue. The English KJV word Profane is written in Hebrew H#2490, חלל, chalal and defined as: To defile oneself ritually, sexually, etc. It originates from a root meaning to perforate or to pierce through.

Notice that the root stem of Chalal is that same double Lamed - לל. Equivalent to the English letter 'L' - Lamed is the letter which symbolizes 'learning – teaching'. The Sages teach that Lamed struggles with dominance verses servitude, thus, the humbled Lamed reaches higher than any other Hebrew letter and as such, the Lamed – or Teacher is subject to pride and more than any other letter or office it has the ability to lead, yoke or teach as a Shepherd or to destroy with a counterfeit yoke as a Hireling does! Isn't that profound? How many leaders or church Pastors do you personally know who struggle in this area?

At this point I want to caution you to pay close attention here! The above phrase - 'Cast him down AS PROFANE...' is indicating that Lucifer was not originally created in this state, so something happened (Remember that Gap Theory?) that caused him to be found *in this condition*, and which resulted in his being cast down! The text plainly states he had profaned – Chalal – (Go back and check this definition a couple of paragraphs earlier) perforated, pierced through the Veil – Boundary – [*Watch this*] which was nothing less than the, **Garment** of Creations' DNA and for that reason, he defiled himself and in doing so, lead astray the nations! There are myriads entrenched in the Elite hierarchy who are themselves guilty of this same defilement!

Darkness the Veil

Is it possible that Darkness – Choshek was that veil, its purpose to keep hidden the DNA or manifest Light – the Living Word of Creation? All the while, protecting it from contamination or impurities? Could our Messiah Yahshua – The Living Word -

have been this Covering or Garment of Darkness – The Choshek who would later come in the frail garment of another body – a fleshy veil of darkness called the body of man and housing the Light of the World? Revealing that same DNA of Creation only to be pierced or perforated - profaned by the Adversary Satan once again in an attempt to compromise the LIGHT?

This theme of DNA is also seen in the Hebrew root letters for the 2nd 'darkness' – Lailah – which again comes from the double-Lamed root of H#3883, לול, luwl, that means to fold back, and also a staircase, a winding stairs, a shaft or enclosed space with steps or a ladder. This forms the criteria for a DNA Helix! Though we briefly touched on this topic earlier, this definition can be quite bewildering to the novice! Why? I'll try to explain.

If you recall, Jacob 'sees' this same Ladder, in Hebrew called a H#5551, סלם, Sullam, shown once again, from the identical double-Lamed root – סלל, salal. It is defined as: To lift up, cast up, elevate or gather, to move to and fro as in a vibrational shaking! I personally believe that Jacob saw the Vibrational DNA Helix of Creation – that same ENTITY who moved over the face of the waters – moved being from the Hebrew - מרחפת, merahephet, a root from H#7363, רחף, rachaph, which indicates to vibrate over. Oh my dear Reader! Can you not see that your words contain a vibrational power that can, not only change you, but your circumstances? Begin now to speak His Word and watch the power unleashed!

For the record, it's noteworthy to consider that those same letters of רחף, arranged differently give us words indicating fruitful, to bud or blossom, to engage or acquire or betroth as a slave woman who is lawfully able to marry into the House! In the Beginning – B'reshiyt – Genesis - the Ruach covenanted with the Womb of the Waters – Mayim to replenish, make fruitful what the Prince of Darkness - Lailah had made tohu v'bohu! Without form and void, waste and desolate, in Hebrew written: Tohu v'bohu is a powerful Prophetic phrase that has a value of

430 – the same as the years of bondage that Israel endured while in Egypt!

Is this hinting that from the time of his having been cast down and from this time forward, the Adversary, Satan, that old devil, would be presented as a counterfeit source of eternal DNA, a clever ruse that would allow him/it to become a source that many today draw from in hopes of securing immortality? By the way, the ladder of Jacob called - Sullam has a numeric value of 130, the same as Semel, an idol or image of a fallen one! The Enemy has a counterfeit – DON'T YOU EVER DOUBT THAT!

As we look closer, and as we regard this 'Lucifer' especially as he is depicted in Isaiah 14:12 where he is called: הילל בן–שחר, Heylel ben-shachar – in the King's English, Lucifer, son of – the morning, we will uncover some obscure and hitherto, hidden clues. As we've shown Heylel has the same letters as 'Lailah'. But, look closer at the phrase: Ben-shachar: Shachar has a value of 508, the same as the Hebrew גרשה, garushah, a unique word from the same root as garas, first seen in Genesis 3:24 where YHVH drives out – garas - the man from Eden. This word means to expel, to cast out, put away, and to divorce. The rearranged letters of Heylel ben-Shachar could read: Lailah ben-garushah – Darkness, the son (Who was) cast out or expelled!

Again, these implications continue to raise a flag and add validity to our premise that there seems to be a powerful, yet clandestine differentiation between Choshek and Lailah: Choshek is intrinsically shown as a covering veil for the Light of Creation, while Lailah in contrast, becomes a counterfeit covering *feigning* light within! A nod toward this speculation is hidden in plain sight in 2Corinthians 11:14 which says: *And no marvel; for Satan himself is transformed into an angel of light.* Incidentally, this verse follows the condemnation of false apostles and those deceitful workers feigning themselves apostles of Messiah!

In confirmation, from our Isaiah 14 text the word Shachar used as a verb means to turn black, to be black (Not as in race) but instead an indication of the heart's condition such as one whose habit is to charm or conjure as the occult world does. The Serpent – Nachash was himself a charmer or conjurer, an enchanter, guilty of twisting the words of Truth.

While we're at it, it's worth noting that on the color spectrum Black is shown not absent color, rather it is the combination of 3-primary colors: Red, Blue and Yellow. Red is depicted as the color of the will and its expression. Blue, the color of the emotions and desire.

Yellow is said to be the color of the mental plane, thereby affecting the mind. In this way, Black, darkness or Lailah – alias Ben Shachar - The Son of the Morning - directly controls or manipulates the fleshly or carnal appetites!

Herein lies a great mystery! Again, let me make it clear: The translators don't seem to draw a distinction between the contrasting forms of 'darkness': For instance; Choshek doesn't mean the absence of Light as in total Blackness, only that Choshek becomes a garment housing, encircling, being worn by the Light or Consuming Fire of Elohiym.

Further, this Choshek Darkness covers *The Light* that is hidden within its folds, much as the Veil or Curtain of the Holy Place separates the Light of the Holy of Holies from the other areas. The Psalmist (18:11) declares: *"...He made darkness His hiding/secret place; His pavilion round about Him were dark waters and thick clouds of the skies.*

**Note the following key words as we decipher them in the Hebrew rather than accepting their innocuous English renderings.

- Secret: H#5643   סתר   *Satar*

    It is a covering, to cloak oneself in secret things.

Curiously, in the book of Job, thought by most to be the oldest of the canonized books, Choshek – darkness is seen a total of 26 times! Here Job and his friends discuss the significance of darkness in the affairs of man. It is mentioned here more than any other book. 26 as a numeric value can be seen representing YHVH! Now, take a closer look back at Psalms 18:11.

- Pavilion, H#5521   סכה   *Sukkah*

    It is a well-known word indicating an enclosed, intimate chamber. It comes from sakak; meaning to cover, overshadow, to stop the approach, to weave or to intertwine. This sukkah or canopy/covering separates the 2nd 'Heaven' – that Throne Room of the King - from the common lower abode of the heavenlies, a boundary established at Creation!

Could this also hint that the Holy Convocations or Festivals found in Leviticus 23 like those such as the Sabbath and Sukkot and Pesach or Passover, could literally become a hiding place, where Thick Darkness covers us while the enemy seeks us out for destruction? How apropos that most Church Christians disparage their sanctity, having fallen prey to the twisted words of the enchanters who follow men's traditions more than those of YHVH. This mindset will shut those places of sanctuary to them much as the blood upon the doorposts of the houses of Israel.

On this evidence, dear Reader, it does seem as if a dual existence, or two distinct entities are being represented in this 9th plague: Choshek-Darkness the covering veil, where the Light of YHVH resides and Lailah-Darkness the place where there is no light or life, only the oppressive form of the enemy! Let's explore this a bit more. This latter darkness seems akin to the 2nd Death – the place where there is the Absence of the Presence of YHVH –The Light – making this the eternal abode of Black, Lailah, and Ben Shachar Darkness!

5 Other Clues Regarding Darkness

- #1 - Our text in Exodus 10:21-23 tells us this Darkness-Choshek could be felt, H#4959, מששׁ, mashash, to feel or touch. The gematria of mashash is 640, the same as משמרכם, mishmarchem, translated as 'your prison', the place where one is guarded or watched. It seems Choshek could both protect what is within its covering as well as, guard it from whom or whatever is outside its enclave. Doesn't this sound like our earlier explanation of the events of Genesis 1 where 'Darkness was upon – guarded – the face of the deep – tehowm?

- #2 – This darkness was a thick darkness: Thick, being from the Hebrew H#653, אפלה, 'aphelah'. Though translated as thick, it also connotes a wretchedness. The 2-letter root, Alef-Pey hints at a girding on or binding, to tie something on the body, as in a band around a person similar to the Ephod worn by the High Priest. Remember, Yahshua is the High Priest after the Order of Melchizedek, yet Lucifer also wore the Ephod in Eden as well!

This darkness literally surrounded each person, tightening around them like a constricting band. This is consistent with the origin of the Alef, out of which both Man (איש) and Fire (אש) are formed!

Consider this crude drawing of the Alef[#22] as a reference! א

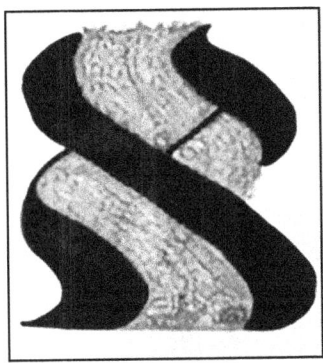

It is the Alef, representing Messiah who girds on, is cloaked with the High Priestly garment of this Choshek/Darkness enveloping the Fire of the Created Man within a protective Veil, while shutting out those outside to thick darkness - wretchedness and death!

Though we may not fully understand this 'Darkness', rest assured we shall experience it again in the near future. Many are looking for the "Day of the Lord -YHVH" and it is coming!

**Note Amos 5:20 *Shall not the day of the Lord Be Darkness, and not light? Even very dark, and no brightness in it?*

- #3 – No one in Egypt saw another, the darkness was so thick that they could not/did not move for 3-days. *They saw not one another, neither rose any from his place for three days: but all the children of Israel had light in their dwellings.* Were they literally 'bound' constricted by the darkness? Held there for 3-days?

**Remember this.

[#22] Drawing of the Alef by David Mathews.

In support of the above, I found it interesting to look at the English phrase; *'neither rose any from his place'* written in Hebrew: מתחתיו, Mitachetaiv, the root being – H#8478, תחת, tachath which indicates 'under, beneath, to depress or press under'.

If we rearrange the letters to form H#2865, חתת, hatat, we have a strong verb expressing severe fright, to be shattered, totally dismayed, scared, terrified and shattered by YHVH. In Revelation 16 these same plagues cause men to gnaw their tongues in agony! Is it possible, while constrained, that some entity tormented them mentally and physically? Perhaps violating them in a manner seen only in Darkness – the Tohu v'bohu – waste and desolate place where the SEED or LIGHT of YHVH is replicated by the Fallen Ones?

The root of tachath comes from תחו, tochu, which indicates abasement, degradation, disgrace, and humiliation. It is very similar etymologically to TOHU as in Tohu V'bohu, only written with the Chet rather than the Hey. Yet it espouses a similar idea as when Creation had been made waste and desolate, abased, degraded while the 1st Darkness – Choshek was upon the Face of the Tehowm, pressing it down, subjecting it!

This plague was indeed horrific! For 3 days no Egyptian could move, societal structure destroyed. Individuals couldn't take care of themselves much less the family or children. No food or water could be had. No comfort of knowing when or if the darkness would lift.

Mental breakdowns are hinted at because a symptom of severe depression is the inability to move! Egypt is placed into solitary confinement. Based on our previous studies, we know that there were horrific previous encounters with great swarms, which we interpreted as hybridized-chimera like beings, a demonic or fallen angelic horde beyond description! Imagine now, being blind and unable to move, perhaps even at the mercy of such!

- #4 - Darkness lasting 3-days? This statement immediately caused electricity to run through me! I immediately thought of Jonah and his 3 - days and 3 - nights inside the belly of the great fish! In the greatest agony Jonah cries out from the belly, (H#990, בטן, beten) of hell, H#7585, שאול, Sheol.

It is this sign of Jonah to which Yahshua makes reference as the only sign of His claim to and proof of, His role as Messiah. Moreover, this same sign is also connected to His 2nd coming. Jonah, H#3123, יונה, in Hebrew is traditionally rendered as 'dove'. Yet we must remember that he is called Jonah son of Amittai, יונה בן–אמתי Yonah ben-Amittai; Amittai means 'My Emet' or My Truth.

Further, the root of Jonah means 'vexor'. Thus, Yahshua could have intended that the Sign of His being Messiah would be when – They Vexed the Son of My Truth! I.E. When they executed Him! Additionally, when the Anti-Messiah appears and attempts to VEX THE OUTCASTS – THE SONS OF MY TRUTH – EXPECT THE KING TO INTERVENE once more with a demonstration of His Claim as Messiah!

Back to the Fish Belly

The English word belly is translated in Hebrew as Beten: Again, rendered belly, or womb, but more literally a hollow and empty place. It derives from the Bet-Tet root that forms words indicating utterance, pronunciation, and expression, to articulate. While the Nun suffixed hints at life, seed. Thus, beten is the place where life is expressed, uttered, articulated!

Sheol, on the other hand, is depicted as the belly of the underworld, the grave or pit, the place full of thick darkness; it actually originates out of sha'al, to ask, enquire, and to beg or to demand. There seems to be a poetic twist here as 'beten Sheol' – the

Belly of Sheol – seems the place where those souls beg, ask or demand to express life! Yet, this DARKNESS doesn't allow for life to express itself! This sounds exactly like what the Egyptians were experiencing! Quite frankly, we're living in a season of darkness when the Powers That Be will not allow the People to express life either! It will only get worse!

Based on this scenario, is it possible that while in Goshen, and while Israel is surrounded and hidden from view, Egypt is taken into the bowels of Sheol and allowed to experience the '2nd-Death' for 3-days?

As we examine each successive definition for 'Darkness', it seems as if we're dealing with 2 distinct types or entities! The Darkness that surrounds and wombs light or life and the darkness of Sheol where no light or life exists! This again, sounds like the 2nd-death!

Likewise, it was this 'Sign of Jonah' that Messiah Yahshua referred to when questioned by the Pharisees.

**Remember, like Pharaoh they are rebuked for seeking a sign. Matthew 12:38 tells us that the Son of Man would be 3-days and 3-nights in the heart of the earth as Jonah was in the Fish. The Zodiacal Sign of the Son of Man is Aquarius, the sign that begins during the middle month of the 3-dark months of winter! Aquarius is 'The Man in the Sea'! Now, let's return to our clues regarding 'Darkness'.

- #5 - Israel had light in their dwellings? This next sentence from Exodus 10:23 is quite engaging. The English reads: ...*but all the children of Israel had light in their dwellings. Ulehchal-beni Yisra'el chayah owr b'moshvotam...*

**Note the word 'chayah' – which is mistranslated as 'had' – however, it could also read 'to exist', to be, became, or to happen. With that in mind, the retranslated verse then gives us: All the children of Israel BECAME light in their dwellings! How could this be? This mystery is quite intriguing, because the New Testament refers to the Believers as 'Children of the Light'. Do you suppose there is a connection? Perhaps a bit more scriptural excavation is called for? Take a look further...

Remember this Darkness is referred to as 'thick' – אפלה, aphelah, the root of which, Alef-Pey-Lamed, is indeed rendered darkness, and can be found related to the two oracular stones hidden within the High Priest's breastplate or Ephod and called 'Urim and Thummim'. Traditionally, these two stones are rendered "lights and perfection". However, many scholars believe the Tet-Mem roots of Thummim are cognate with those of the Tav-Mem root stems that hint at concealing, specifically, that which is hidden – as in DARKNESS! Making these two stones – LIGHTS/FIRE AND DARKNESS INSTEAD! Utterly remarkable and yet consistent with all we've discussed thus far!

As we continue, many scholars believe these two stones were in stark contrast with one another. For example: Light versus Darkness. However, it seems that the idea is more of a symbiotic relationship such as: Light within Darkness! In other words, Light that is hidden or concealed within the Darkness. Therefore, Israel (The Light) and their destiny are hidden within this Plague. Many times we endure trials, hardships, etc. and become cynical or get frustrated thinking that we're suffering unnecessarily. However, Jeremiah 29:11 reminds us that YHVH has plans for us, plans for good and not for evil, to bring us to an expected destination. Though these plagues surely didn't look like a beneficial plan to Israel, it is without doubt in hindsight, that they were part of the sifting process required to distinguish Wheat from Tares! Moreover, most Believers fail to make the above connections because of having been separated from an understanding of the Message of Redemption written in the stellar luminaries. Yet, the Pagans are fully aware of and take advantage of their message. Why can't we see the truth and acknowledge their import? For example? The 12-Stones of the Breastplate worn by the High Priest represent the 12-Tribes, 12-Months and 12-Zodiacal Houses. While the Urim and Thummim represent the Primordial Light of creation and point us back toward the Genesis record revealing the Garment that clothed or housed it – Choshek – Darkness!

In keeping with this, the Body of Messiah is also finding their destiny in the midst of these future Plagues! While the world succumbs to such darkness those who do know their Elohiym will do great exploits!

Israel during this plague thus, begins a unique transformation; taking on the form or being absorbed within/clothed with the Darkness - they become the Light of the World garbed in a fleshly form! Yahshua remarks about this transformation in Matthew 5:14 where, during His dissertation on Kingdom Principles, He is found declaring the Lost Sheep of the House of Israel as *"the Light of the World"*. It seems that during these plagues Israel is experiencing a 'Resurrection' of sorts, a season of death, burial and resurrection, while Egypt finds themselves in the throes of death with no hope!

Again, for the sake of repetition it seems darkness takes on two forms during this plague: Choshek, who protects Israel, enveloping them while forming a protective shield against the tormentor who resides in the Lailah darkness that wreaks havoc in Egypt!

Before we move on and for the record, this same Being whom I believe to have been none other than Yahshua in the form of this Choshek 'Darkness' who later accompanies Israel out of Egypt is seen standing between the two enemies once more:

> Exodus 14:19,20 *And the angel of YHVH, which went before the camp of Israel, removed and went behind them; and the pillar of the cloud went from before their*

face, and stood behind them: And it came between the camp of the Egyptians and the camp of Israel; and it was a cloud and Darkness to them, but it gave light by night to these: so that the one came not near the other all the night!

The last verse of Exodus 14:19,20 has a grammatical break where the Pillar of Cloud comes between the two camps. The word for cloud, H#6051, ענן, pronounced 'anan' can be translated as a covering or veil. Accordingly, the Hebrew could read: הענן ויאר והחשך את-הלילה h`anan v'yeor ve'hahosek Et-lailah. The Pillar is depicted as showing the direct object here 'lailah' and is written as את (The ET-Alef Tav) who became a covering veil for the Light *against the Lailah*. The phrase 'To Them' and 'To these' is not in the original text'. Therefore, it is my opinion that it was the Choshek-Darkness also known as the Light-Life who stood between the two Camps and did not allow the Lailah-Darkness-Death to come nigh the Camp of Israel!

What Does the Future 9th Plague Look Like?

If what we've seen continues and it is evident these are generational patterns, the coming 'Tribulation' plague of darkness could follow the above Exodus example, as well as, reveal to us a unique twist that will fit these uncertain times. How so? Let me stipulate: I am NOT POLITICAL. BUT THE FOLLOWING BEARS SCRUTINY!

The Biblical texts are rife with reference to the Stellar Luminaries being darkened and even the prophet Zachariah speaks of a thermo-nuclear event that could lead to a "Nuclear Winter" or man-made darkness. Further, we're experiencing cataclysmic weather patterns that I personally believe to be manipulated by EMF – electromagnetic frequencies and directed energy weapons. I firmly believe the latter left a telltale grid-like signature during the great California and Oregon fires of 2020

The Exodus Keys

revealing those events to have been influenced beyond the random patterns left by an ordinary forest fire. Could such intentional manipulation as this lead us down a spiraling tunnel into the "LONG DARK WINTER" SPOKEN OF BY JOE BIDEN during 2020? Ironically, he wasn't the first to coin the phrase: Dark Winter was a government Bioterrorism Exercise held at Andrews Air Force base June 22-23, 2001: June = 6. 22+23+21 = 666.

Though many may discard the following, it's not an accident that his presidential slogan was: **B**uild **B**ack **B**etter – the letter '**B**' the only English letter capable of hiding the #**6,** while his surname Biden hints at iden-tity, thus B – **666 iden**tity.

In addition, behind his personal campaign slogan – where he clearly remarks that there's a battle for the Soul of the Nation - he also asked people to text 'UNITED' to 30330 during his campaign and while actually calling himself: Joe 30330: Further, 2020 divided by 666 = 3.0330. Ironically, the gematria of UNITED = 358, is the same as both Nachash and Mashiach! The Hebrew word for UNITED is מאוחד, me'uchad, and its value of 59 is the same as Niddah: An unclean or abominable act requiring removal or separation. Coincidence? You make the call. Again, I didn't vote for either candidate and have no political dog in the fight so to speak. I am however, required to share the prophetic insight that I believe Abba is giving me and do not apologize.

Now, though it may seem a serendipitous choice on the part of this author, I would have you note Matthew 6:22,23 in particular that it shares the same numbers as the date of the Bio-Terrorism event (Dark Winter) of June 22-23. *The light of the body is the eye: if therefore thine eye by single, thy whole body shall be full of light. But, if thine eye be evil, thy whole body shall be full of darkness. If therefore the light that is in thee be darkness, how great is that darkness!*

Further, you might point out that it seems very convenient that we're once again speaking of darkness in this verse! The Greek word used here is <u>Greek. #4652</u> skot-i-nos; is a word that indicates to be covered with darkness! This word comes from the root <u>Greek. #4639</u> 'skia' hinting at an image cast by an object and therefore, representing its form: Much like the Shadow of a looming presence. Skia is cognate with <u>Gk. #4633</u>, Skene, a tent, tabernacle, and a dwelling. A Skin vessel whose shadow casts a form of its presence!

As we discussed above, the connection between darkness – blackness and שחר shachar indicates that the Lailah associated with Heylel points toward the Red, Blue and Yellow colors or their vibrational – FREQUENCIES.

(**Remember: Red is depicted as the color of the will and its expression. While Blue the color of the emotion and desire. Yellow on the other hand is said to be the color of the mental plane, affecting the mind.) If true then surely we must realize that the worldwide attempt by the Elite to irradiate the planet and the People with such vibrational frequencies has an end-goal: And that objective is to completely obscure and control the MIND! Sounds like a plague of Darkness doesn't it?

For our record here, it is also worth noting that you don't have to "see" darkness or light in order to be affected by it. How so? The Skin is stimulated by colors (Dr. Kurt Goldstein neuropsychologist).

**Remember Skene, skia or skin tent from above?

Therefore, this Long, Dark, Winter could involve the launch of a plague of Darkness affecting the Minds, Will and intellect of the People! To corroborate this, Science has concluded that changes in gene expression are seen following EMF exposure (WIFI, cell phones, smart meters, baby monitors, etc) in as little as just 2-hours!

In summation, I believe this future Great Tribulation Plague is literally a "BATTLE FOR THE MINDS OR SOUL OF THE PEOPLE". One group will be protected by the Choshek darkness that envelops them defending the Light that is within them: In other words, those who have not *conformed to this world but have been transformed by the renewing of their minds* (Romans 12:2) will have/become – like the Children of Israel - the LIGHT IN GOSHEN!

In contrast, those who conform to the world – the Lailah darkness – will become more debased, more susceptible to the devices of the enemy, while finding themselves in utter torment like never before!

This Greek word used in Romans 12 for 'conform' – Gk#4964, syschematizo comes from a compound of syn and schema: The former indicates an intimate UNION while the latter means to take on the nature, character, and constitution, especially the physical build, in other words the very likeness! Could this indicate another future UNION with the SEED of DARKNESS being planted in the Womb of their minds, thereby, producing offspring of the sort seen in Genesis 6 and following? By the way, let me say emphatically - There is no repentance found for this group of mutations or Nephylim! Be forewarned dear Reader there are indeed Dark Days ahead for many!

Could this same scenario have first been shown to have happened to Egypt during the plague of 'Thick Darkness'? Again, thick being from the Hebrew word אפלה, aphelah, the same root as Ephod. Israel takes on the Ephod - Garment of Thick Darkness that YHVH dwells in and becomes the Firstborn of YHVH while Egypt is conformed to the counterfeit Ephod or priestly breastplate depicted as having been worn by the Fallen Lailah darkness and missing the Breastplate stones of Redemption! Take a look here for confirmation found at:

> Ezekiel 28:14 *Thou art the anointed cherub that covereth; and I have set these so: thou wast upon the holy mountain of YHVH; thou hast walked up and down in the midst of the stones of fire.*

In conclusion of our look at the 9th Plague of Darkness I'll leave you with the following couple of verses pointing to what lies ahead for those of the Greater Exodus!

> Revelation 16:10 *And the fifth angel poured out his vial upon the seat of the beast; and his kingdom was full of darkness; and they gnawed their tongues for pain,*

Like what took place between Pharaoh, Egypt and Israel, this is a battle between Kingdoms: The Throne of the Beast against that of the Messiah. You can take courage My Friend because this will not take The Creator by surprise. Stand fast in Him and remember this:

> Ephesians 6:12 *For we wrestle not against flesh and blood, but against principalities, against powers, against* **the rulers of the darkness of this world**, *against spiritual wickedness in high places.*

Lastly, the Apostle John says Men love darkness rather than light. **Darkness** is *"skotos"* in Greek and means *"blindness, ignorance and an obscurity that leads to unrighteousness and ungodliness."* Satan and other Fallen Ones exert their control through the ignorance, blindness and ungodliness of the Masses, perpetuating the darkness in this world.

Will you become the Light in your Dwelling when the Darkness comes? I challenge you to search your hearts in this season of relative ease. We have been challenged to reach higher, do more, and draw closer. You have picked up this book and have read this far simply because it is an instrument that Abba is using to prick your heart in preparation for what He has planned for you! The road you've taken to get here has been fraught with difficulty. But, let me remind you dear Reader. You've known for some time that you were chosen for this hour. You are being called to a deeper walk in order to prepare you to become that Beacon of Light on the shores of despair and hardship. There will be many who will become shipwrecked on the hidden rocks of disillusion found in their religious traditions. Many Charismatic Leaders within the Church will be found calling for their followers to abandon the Ship of the Ancient Text of Scripture. You dare not! Stay the course! Trust in Him! Now, take a deep breath and let's go on to the next chapter dealing with the 10th plague: Death of the Firstborn.

Chapter 11

The 10ᵗʰ Plague: Death of the Firstborn[23]

Exodus 11:1-10, 12:51

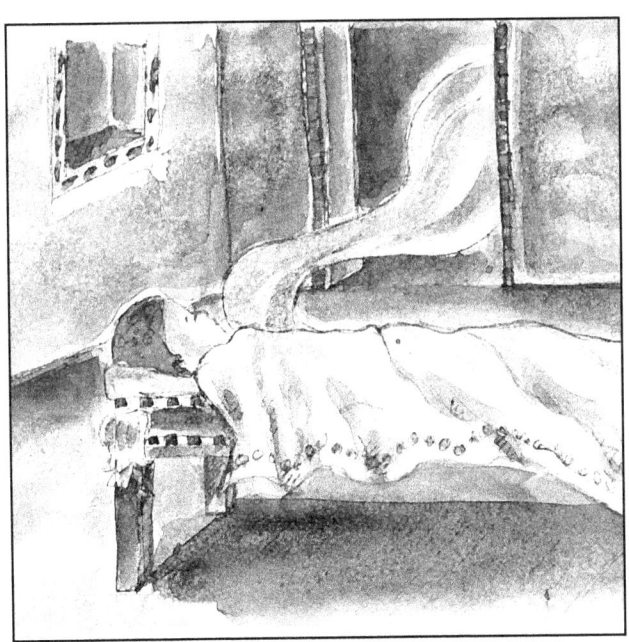

This plague is probably the most familiar of all the Exodus encounters as it is connected to Pesach or Passover, which from the text in Chapter 12 we know begins at sundown the 13ᵗʰ of the Hebrew month of Nissan (March-April) and ends sundown the 14ᵗʰ while the Festival of Unleavened Bread begins at sundown

---

[23] Sabine Alex http://www.torah-illustrations.blogspot.com/
Used with permission.

at the end of the 14th and the beginning the 15th and ends 7-days later at sundown on the 22nd. What is quite interesting is the timing of this former event of Passover coupled with the aforementioned 9th Plague of Darkness!

**Note: First, bear in mind that much controversy surrounds the following supposition as any remote connection to Yahshua as the Pesach/Passover Lamb had to be avoided by all Jewish commentators.

Now, pay attention to Exodus 12:3 where Israel is commanded to bring a lamb into their house on the 10th of Nissan and where, for 4-days it is examined by the household. This occurs at the same time that the National Lamb is examined until such time the Priest declares *"I find no fault in him"* where it is then slaughtered *'between the evenings'* on the 14th. Perhaps you'll recall Yahshua being questioned vociferously by the Priests on the Temple Mount for the same consecutive 4-days until His arrest, trial and sentencing where Pilot also declares: "I find no fault in Him". This begins a 3-day period where Yahshua is in the bowels of Sheol until the evening of the 17th, a set-time that also happens to be a minor festival called "Yom H'Bikkurim" or early first fruits! Fulfilling to the minute the 3-days and 3-nights of the Sign of Jonah!

In addition, from the account of Abraham in Genesis 17 and 18, we can see another parallel of the Passover account. At this instance, here we find Abraham and the men of his house have been recently circumcised on the 10th. Three days later, he is again seen sitting under the Oak of Mamre whereupon the Messiah appears with 2 angels. Again, to corroborate our position we find that Abraham sends for a lamb of the flock as he prepares the Pesach meal for his angelic visitors.

Against this backdrop and in opposition to our position, some would argue that the cycle of keeping the Festivals did not occur until the accounts of Exodus 12. However, upon closer scrutiny of the Torah from Genesis 3 forward if we look at the Hebrew language we can find irrefutable proof that the Festivals were not only known, but adhered to by Adam, Cain and Abel, Noah, Abraham and others! Point of fact: The murder of Abel by his brother Cain takes place at Pesach. So, what does this prove, if anything? Well, most Believers have no clue regarding the time-keeping device that is the Stellar Luminaries or Zodiacal Signs whose sole purpose (Genesis 1:14) is to regulate the Moedim or Holy Convocations. The events of Exodus 12 were to recalibrate the calendar of Israel after several cataclysmic events that led to calendar changes. If you have questions here please take a look at my earlier book entitled: *Ezekiel's Wheel Within A Wheel* (CCB Publishing). You'll find sufficient evidence to support the above. In the meantime, let's proceed.

As we continue to look at Exodus 12 it seems reasonable that Israel would have followed the same pattern in order to fulfill the Moedim's commandment. Thus, it is my opinion that the Plague of darkness that lasted 3-days would have congruently, not only with the circumcision of Abraham and his house, but also with the Circumcision of Israel which I contend began on the 10th and ending or lifted afterwards on the 14th in perfect time for the Blood of the Pesach Lamb to be applied to their door posts.

This would have been the consummate 'cover' because during any other ordinary time where there was a need for the healing of Israel, Pharaoh's workload was such that it would not have allowed Israel 3-days off work, as in this case, had it not been for the Plague of darkness occurring just prior to the slaughter of the First Born. Does this make sense to you?

On the other hand, neither would they have been able to walk out of Egypt if they had indeed been circumcised 3-days later at that same Pesach evening (According to the Rabbis) an event which would have easily been refuted by the words of:

Psalms 105:37 *He brought them forth also with silver and gold: and there was not one* **feeble** *person among their tribes.*

Feeble comes from the Hebrew word H#3782, כשל, kawshal, to stumble, be feeble, weak, to be injured, especially a weakness of the legs.

Let's Take A Side Trip Here

The Hebrew word Kawshal has a gematria of 350, the same as that found in the Hebrew word H#6083, עפר, `aphar and which, is rendered 'dust'. `Aphar can be first seen in Genesis 2:7 where Adam is said to have been formed of 'the *dust* of the Adamah'! The KJV English Translators struggle with the origin of `aphar, defining it as 'dust, fine particles, dry, and powder'.

However, we can glean more from the context – i.e. that of Adam being formed, יצר, yatsar, squeezed, formed or fashioned – from the dust of the Adamah a term which, seems to indicate that `aphar was the residue of the Adamah, itself an interesting word whose root, 'dam' specifically indicates blood; thus prior to the fall the dam or blood had unique physiological properties and as such, would have been seen as a type of *light-substance housing the life* – The DNA or building blocks of creation! (Leviticus 17:11 *...the life of the flesh is in the blood...*) as a result, Israel, following the pattern would have left Egypt in a regenerated condition, born again if you will. The result of which we find circumcision becoming the outward physical sign of the cutting off of the dead flesh!

Now, before we get too far ahead of ourselves we need to readdress the 10th plague and frame it according to context within the scope of the previous 9-plagues.

Death of the 1ˢᵗ Born

We all know that YHVH doesn't mince words. Therefore, the choice of the words in Exodus 11:1 is notable: And YHVH said unto Moshe: עוֹד נֶגַע אֶחָד אָבִיא עַל־פַּרְעֹה וְעַל־מִצְרַיִם ... 'od nega 'echad 'avi 'al-Paroh v'al-Mitsrayim... The KJV renders this 'Yet I will bring one more plague upon Pharaoh and upon Egypt...' However, the intentional use of the word 'nega' indicates this to be the 1ˢᵗ-time or 1ˢᵗ strike of this sort. The Hebrew H#5061, נֶגַע, nega, meaning a strike or blow, a mark or spot as in leprosy and to lay the hand upon. Moreover, in a surprising twist *it also points toward lying with a woman carnally*. More on this in a few...

In the text, Nega is preceded by a peculiar word written עוֹד, 'OD. Though translated by the KJV as a preposition it can also indicate 'to witness', to certify or testify. By connecting our extrapolated definitions of both words: 'Od and nega – something entirely different is seen because now the verse could read: And YHVH said unto Moshe *"Testify or certify of the sexual immorality and I will bring one Strike or Plague upon Pharaoh and Egypt"*!

In view of our theory, then we must ask ourselves did Moshe perhaps have access to critical information that could be condemning to both Egypt and Pharaoh? Surely you recall that Moshe was raised as half-brother to this same Pharaoh and privy to information that only a person of his former stature could have accessed!

I want to admonish you to pay close attention here to נֶגַע, as the Hebrew word Nega has the same letters as H#6026, עֹנֶג, Oneg, meaning 'delight' and which, is used to describe the Shabbat or Sabbath. In that context Oneg does indeed mean delight. However, more appropriately, it describes what is characterized as; the alluring, enticing and romantically amorous appeal of women. This fervent desire or passion was intentionally created by YHVH and given to the Man-Adam for his Woman-Ishshah and solely intended for that Union!

Hence the reason for the Sabbath being called the 'Bride'; that we might delight – Oneg - ourselves in YHVH! (Please see Isaiah 58:14) To contravene the intent of that Sanctified as Holy Union, means that what was once a 'delight' now becomes a curse and invokes a NEGA – Plague – Strike from YHVH upon that union! The same can be said for not keeping the Sabbath! Is there a connection to this strike being launched perhaps against the firstborn – offspring of what perhaps could have been an illicit sexual union that Moshe knew about?

Allow me to get a bit esoteric for a moment. It is evident that YHVH viewed sexual immorality as an abomination. For all intents and purposes, in this context here in Exodus, Israel stands in the same place as Adam: In fact, Israel is referred to as the 'firstborn' son of YHVH and much like the first Adam created in His (YHVH's) image. This sets a precedent that continues from Genesis 1 forward where the intent of The Creator is for the Firstborn to produce sons of YHVH in His image in order to continue His Great Name.

In this vein, Adam was created with the ability to 'reproduce' by speaking – in effect, wording sons into being! It is only *after the fall* that the fleshly or carnal view of sexual reproduction takes place. Further, anything outside the confines of the sacred Union/Marriage of the one - Echad Man and the one - Echad Woman results in a curse/plague/nega upon the union! Man was intended to delight – Oneg in, his own wife. In Genesis 3 we find the Nachash or Serpent compromising this order.

Despite anything to the contrary, this sets into motion a carnal lust circumventing the original sanctity of this Oneg-Delight – and instead we find this carnal appeal becoming an issue that caused both the first Egyptian Pharaoh and later Abimelech to pursue Sarai and Rebekah. We'll look closer here...and I know you're concerned that I forgot about the 10th plague, but, remember we're establishing a foundation for motive and showing context for the purpose that you are enable to see things that most cannot!

Notwithstanding, the ability to produce Sons in the Image of YHVH is the bridge between the spiritual and physical, that bridge is the foundation upon which creation sits. The Mystics call this the Yesod, the 9th sephirah or node of the Tree of Life. Let me remind you of the Hebrew word עוד, `OD – to witness or certify, testify – it has a gematria of 80, the same as יסוד, Yesod! Thus, this evidence seems to convey that this Exodus NEGA is a direct result of sexual abomination!

We Have to Look Closer Here at This Latter Hypothesis!

This position of ours is engrossing to say the least. The law of first reference finds this word 'Nega' initially used in Genesis 12:17 to describe the events that took place when another Pharaoh took Abram's wife Sarai into his house. Unfortunately, tradition has clouded our perspective of this incident, which, I believe, leads to a precedent setting, serious release of great plagues (nega) upon this first Pharaoh and Egypt because of Sarai Abram's wife. Framed from this precedent perhaps it will reveal more of why this particular word is used in Exodus 11? Before continuing, I must ask you a sobering question. One that will surely rankle many of the 'traditionalists' who refuse to think outside the box of Talmudic interpretation or the poorly translated English commentaries.

Did the Genesis 12 account find Pharaoh lying sexually with Sarai? Did I hear a collective gasp? Most dare not consider this! Yet, we want the truth right?

To form a preface to our answer, we state unequivocally that Scripture mandates that at least two, preferably three witnesses be provided before one cites a doctrinal or theological maxim. That being said, aside from Genesis 12 there are at least 2 other accounts (Witnesses?) of similar instances where a 'Sister/Wife' scenario occurs: First, we have Genesis 20:1-18 and another incident with Abram and Sarai, where we're told categorically that Abimelech did not have sex with Sarah and secondly, in Genesis 26:6-11 we find a 'like father like son' scenario where Isaac – is found posing the same as Abram – as the 'brother' of Rebekah, she who, as a result, is also taken into Abimelech's house.

In these 2 latter cases, the text makes it plain that nothing happened! Though in both the latter cases it is also unquestionably made known to Pharaoh and Abimelech *before an incident occurs*, that extra-marital sex would result in a serious plague – BUT SUCH WARNING IS NOT GIVEN TO THE PHARAOH IN GENESIS 12? Heeding the warning the plagues promised in the other 2-examples do not happen, yet in this first case of Abram, Sarai and Pharaoh they do! Why? YHVH is a fair judge. Though I'll probably be attacked by many for saying so, it seems highly likely that Sarai did indeed sleep with Pharaoh!

In reality, as we examine this first account of Genesis 12 it parallels the Exodus account rather remarkably! For instance, as with Moshe, Abram is called to stand before Pharaoh. Additionally, the theme of both is that of a "letting go": First of Abram and Sarai and later, Israel. The phrase 'let go' is translated from the Hebrew word Shalach, H#7971, to send away, let loose and to be ***divorced***! Is it possible that by taking Sarai into his harem across the threshold that an Egyptian marriage ceremony occurred causing an adulterous situation? Skeptical yet?

**By way of reminder: The ancient Threshold Ceremony – in which, the carrying of one's bride across - was seen as public declaration of a marriage!

Another interesting connection to which the Sages somewhat allude, is that Sarai was also known as Iscah based on the interpretation of:

> Genesis 11:29: *And Abram and Nahor took them wives: The name of Abram's wife was Sarai; and the name of Nahor's wife, Milcah, the daughter of Haran, the father of Milcah and the father of Iscah.*

This begs our indulgence for a moment. Making these assumptions leads me to believe that the Sages or Rabbis knew a bit more than they're willing to say regarding the potential of the Grand Matriarch of Israel having her virtue called into question! Watch this!

- Iscah, H#3252   יסכה   *Yischa*

  Translated as "One who looks forth" or Sees. To watch. However, the root stem is notable: Samech-Kaf-Hey gives us Sukkah. As a noun it indicates a covering or hiding place. Yet the Psalmist uses its verbal form in Psalms 139:13 *For thou hast possessed my reins: thou hast covered-H#5526, סכך, sakak, me in my mother's womb.*

- Sakak in its verbal form hints at the formation or weaving of a baby in the womb. As a young woman the prophetic name of Yischa hints that she could then 'SEE' – Prophesy of the Promised Seed to be formed in her womb. This seed was to be the Promised Seed or Firstborn much like Israel would later be the Firstborn of

YHVH. Thus anointed, and armed with such foreknowledge, any compromise with Pharaoh would have resulted in a NEGA – Strike just as in Genesis 3!

This is also ostensibly confirmed when YHVH changes both Abram and Sarai's names, adding the Hebrew letter "Hey – ה" which indicates breath, breathing, mouth, spirit and revelation. When you transliterate ה into English you have אה– an exclamatory word meaning 'See! Behold! Surely! To bring emphasis to something being declared! It seems YHVH is correcting the way Sarai 'SEES'! Her subsequent Name change means an emphatic status change!

Side Bar - The Shalach Connection

Earlier, we spoke to you about the phrase that was consistent in both Genesis 3, Genesis 12, and the Exodus – letting go – Shalach. I thought it would help you some if I put this in a bit more perspective and then we'll come back here.

It is worth noting here that the Torah Parsha (The Weekly Scriptural cycle) entitled V'Yishlach – And He Went Out – comes from the above root – shalach. This Torah portion or parsha reminds us of the ancient archenemy of Israel: Amalek, a grandson of Esau. This was the lineage that despised the Birthright. The Firstborn! Esau was cut off from his inheritance, as was the firstborn of Egypt. In keeping with the character of his grandfather, it was Amalek who first made war against Israel after the Exodus, preying on the weak and elderly at the back of the camp.

**Note: During this battle with Amalek Israel is able to win only if Moshe's hands are held aloft by his servants (Implying an acknowledged return to Torah) Aaron and Hur.

Their names give us: The One Who carries/wombs the Light and the Burning One respectively. This takes place while Joshua – Yahshua fights the Battle!

The battle is fought at Rephidim, H#7508, and רפידים, is translated 'rests' or stays, which is a poor KJV translation and more literally means balusters or stair supports. This, I believe was the location of Jacob's vision of the Stair or ladder – the DNA of Creation. Rephidim comes from the root rapah, indicating to reinvigorate, to restore, bring to life and is associated with Giants or Nephylim!

In the near future, prior to what we're calling the Greater Exodus, we will see a battle over this same DNA of Creation, while the Powers That Be are found making the attempt to replicate or restore the DNA of the Fallen Ones! This hybridized concoction that cannot co-exist with the DNA or Word of YHVH will be incorporated into weaponized vaccines and launched through various methods like cloud seeding or Chemtrails and assorted Electro Magnetic Frequencies as Amalek seeks to destroy the weak and elderly first! As we speak (May 2021) in the aftermath of the Greatest World Wide hoax, the Covid-19 pandemic, nations have contrived methods to convince the Mass public to accept these diabolic cocktails! Many of our elderly and infirm and thousands of others have died, others reporting various ailments related to this injection. It will only get worse as the Gene Pool of most families taking the poison are forever changed!

Let's look back at this location called Rephidim. It has a numeric value of 344, the same as H# 5614, סרד, sephard, defined as meaning exiled, separated, to be cast out. From this we get Sephardic, the root of which is Sepher – Book! People of the Book! This is the season when the Maqowm – also known as - The Place of Separation - becomes more visible as the struggle over the Firstborn inheritance escalates! By the way, the Sephardic Peoples are those whom I believe can literally trace a

The Exodus Keys

bloodline connection to Israel, rather than having been 'converted' to Judaism.

As we continue, out of the Amalekite nation comes Agag, their King, a Giant whose name אגג, A- Gog, seems to mean 'from the top' or the apex. Ironically, this root is seen in Exodus 30:3 as denoting the top – H#1406, גג, gag, of the Altar of Incense. Daniel speaks metaphorically of a male goat (ESAU?) in relation to (Gog and Magog) whose one horn becomes four horns stretching towards the four winds of heaven, which, I believe rather than 4-nations, seems to infer instead the four compass points or horns upon a worldwide altar. (Daniel 8:8) Fashioned like the 4-horns of the altar in the 3rd –

Temple this seems instead a euphemism pointing to the worldwide alliance of the world's religious Triad: Jews, Christians and Islam.

Along these lines, it should come as no surprise that Amalek now occupies the 2nd-highest office of the corporate UNITED STATES OF AMERICA at present and will probably soon occupy the 1st: Kamala = Amalek. Again, I'm only presenting evidence that you as the Reader can refute if felt led. I have no political aim with my point.

Now, as we've discussed in our previous teachings on these plagues, the Fallen Angelic and/or Demonic Beings that the Ancients held to be 'gods' enthralled Pharaoh both and the Egyptian nation. With this in mind, it is my opinion that Pharaoh and Egypt engaged in a literal seed transfer that resulted in their producing offspring from that unholy union! Again, the literalist will not see what I'm sharing with you. I pray that your heart has been seasoned and you're prepared for what is coming!

To support in fact my position, the language of Genesis 6 and that of Genesis 12 bear striking similarities in their description of how the Nephylim and the Egyptians perceived the daughters of men and with regard to Sarai and Rebekah. Please note the following phrases consistent to both texts: Then you decide.

**Note 3 partial excerpts below.

And it was when – saw how lovely/beautiful – took – this latter word took, is H#3947, לקח, laqach, translated as 'to seize, acquire, marry, to take a wife, and take possession of.' Is it possible that an event similar to that of Genesis 6 is taking place here as well, with the intent to compromise the SEEDLINE promised through Abraham?

**Remember Sarah is approximately 25-30 years younger at this time than when Isaac is born and yet, here for some reason (*Sarcasm mine*) her womb will be made barren all these years! Why would The Creator allow her to be mocked for her barren condition? Did she merit it? Did YHVH intervene to prevent potential offspring resulting from a compromise in her case? May I remind you, barrenness was often seen as a curse related to adultery (Numbers 5:11-31) though not in every instance?

Following this line of thought it helps us to put into perspective what has always troubled me and that's how Sarah was able to convince Abraham to take an *Egyptian* woman – Hagar – as his wife. Most scholars will argue it was simply the Ancient Near Eastern custom. If so, then why would Sarah do so and later change her mind? To aid us a bit here, though the etymology of the name Hagar escapes most scholars. We found as we dug a bit deeper that it seems the letter Hey attached to the Gimmel-Resh of Hagar -הגר, can function as a preposition giving us 'the' while the Gimmel-Resh derives from gerar, indicating to press into service, forcible servitude, to drag out or away. If so, her name indicates that a subtle objective unseen by most was to bring the Abrahamic lineage into forced servitude by compromising the Seed or bloodline and thus, the Inheritance!

Furthermore, there is a close cognate to Hagar, seen with the identical letters: גרה, gerah, meaning to inflame, to be angry. The verbal form means to strive or agitate strife, obviously not by means of one singular assault but rather by repeated provocations and withdrawals. Ironically, the gematria of Hagar is the same as that of Isaac – 208. Was this to be a counterfeit? Was this one act of many in the retribution of Sarah against Egypt and Abram perhaps? Was it also merely coincidental that Abimelech, who took Sarai captive after Pharaoh, was called the King of Gerar, as in the above sentences of this paragraph?

To help me substantiate this further, it is patently evident that the 10th-plague – Death of the First Born – was undoubtedly the plan of YHVH from the moment He first spoke to Moshe in Exodus 4. Why? What had happened over the past 430-years to cause YHVH to take such drastic measures? To sew this together a bit tighter let's travel a side road…

Another Side Bar

Once more, let me call your attention to the central phrase of our text in this chapter: `Od nega – specifically `Od – עוד whose numeric value of 80 we connected to the word Yesod יסוד, indicating a foundation or base. Remember? This word was used earlier to indicate the base of the Altar where the blood of sacrifices was poured.

Incidentally, the number 430 above also connects us back to this Altar foundation, because the sacrificed 'animal soul' or Nephesh is associated with this same Yesod. Is it possible that the future 3rd-Temple Altar will receive the compromised DNA – blood of Chimera or hybridized animals consistent with Gene manipulation that is intended to reintroduce the Nephylim and/or other monstrosities? Remember the Anti-Messiah will offer Pigs' flesh upon this very Yesod - foundation. When most contemplate this profanation of the 'Temple' it is with regard to the common assumption of Religious Traditionalists that he's doing so in great antipathy toward the Jews. But, is he really? Could what we've presented thus far indicate something much more sinister? Brace yourself and please hear me out before answering!

Throughout history a great paradox has existed regarding the prohibition of Swine's flesh. Even today most Christians treat it as having been made clean by Jesus and routinely dismiss it. However, the reality is that Torah expressly forbade its consumption, yet early Christian records indicate that not only did they consume it, they offered it on their holy days; i.e. Easter Ham! Such conduct exposes a brazen effrontery that is both anti-Semitic and anti-Torah! But, why is pig flesh or swine considered such an abomination and what does it have to do with our 10th Plague?

Here's where we touch something I've not seen before. Swine comes from the Hebrew word H#2386, חזיר, khazeer, translated as swine, yet its root indicates to enclose, to come back, to return, its origin is seen also in words indicating sight, to forecast, prophecy, vision, etc. It is always linked to 'abomination' H#8262, שקץ, shawkats, which is translated as 'to loathe, pollute, to be filthy and to be IMPURE' and in itself represents an ALTERNATE PRIESTHOOD founded by Rome/Esau!

Further, the root Chet-Zayin-Yod-Resh is cognate with Kaf-Zayin-Yod-Resh. Khazar, The plural form being Khazarim. It is often postulated that most Ashkenazi Jews are descended from this group. The name Ashkenazi derives from the Son of Gomer, the son of Japheth, in effect a prophetic fulfillment of Genesis 9:27 which see: *YHVH shall enlarge Japheth, and he shall dwell in the tents of Shem; and Canaan shall be his Servant.* Indeed, the Sons of Japheth – the Ashkenazi Peoples do in fact; now dwell in the Shemitic tents!

**NOTE! For comparison's sake one of Japheth's sons was also named MAGOG!

As we continue, the Shin-Qoph of shawkats gives us a root-stem that is cognate with the Samech-Kaf root of Tabernacle/Sukkah. It is my opinion that Esau now masquerades as Jacob in an attempt to usurp the Birthright! The 10th plague dealt with those usurpers who thought to access the Firstborn birthright of Israel! The Plagues of the Greater Exodus will do the same though on a much larger and horrific scale!

Like Egypt, YHVH will judge the imposters of Esau/Rome who themselves will fulfill Nebuchadnezzar's vision of the 'Iron mixed with Miry clay' and by such devious means attempt to occupy Israel's Firstborn status! By the way, in passing, Khazeer-Swine has a value of 225, the same as *h'nephylim*, and *'because of them'* the phrase used to reference the earth being filled with violence (From 'Them' – the Nephylim or Giants) as the reason given explaining why YHVH would need to destroy the inhabitants of the earth in Genesis 6. This is worth calling attention to. Because throughout Torah whenever YHVH killed men, women and children (And Cattle) as this Firstborn plague would most assuredly do, it was always linked to His judgment upon the compromised SEEDLINE of the Fallen Ones!

In View of This

Was the intent of YHVH to judge this Exodus Pharaoh as He had the nemesis of Abram and Sarai? Did the Exodus Pharaoh comprise the Bride of YHVH – Israel – in a sexual manner and thus, merit the destruction of the seed of that union? Evidence is far more than circumstantial in my opinion! Notice how YHVH instructs Moshe:

**See Exodus 4:22-23 *And thou shalt say unto Pharaoh, Thus saith YHVH, Israel is my son, even my firstborn: And I say unto thee, let my son go, that he may serve me: and if thou refuse to let him go, behold, I will slay thy son, even thy firstborn.*

Look at the Hebrew word for 'slay': H#2026, הרג, rendered hawrag, and is translated here as to slay or kill. It's interesting to note the 2-letter root stem Hey-Resh, rendered 'mountain', a mound and figuratively indicating a 'rounded abdomen' as in a pregnant woman. The Gimmel is the 'lifted up' letter, the by-product or 1st-born son of the union of Alef & Bet.

Its (Hawrag's) gematria – 208 – is the same as Isaac, the 1st-born of Abraham and Sarah and also known as the Promised Seed! Again, was there a hidden Egyptian attempt to eradicate the House of Abraham-Isaac-Jacob by comingling their seed: A seedline that seems clearly to have been abominably tainted with that of the Nephylim!

Further, the other 9-Plagues seemed as if they were supplemental additions to the ultimate 10th plague judgment upon Egypt – shown here as a specific strike upon Pharaoh, the representative of Egypt, as well as, the entire Nation of Egypt – in this 10th event. Why? Again, it seems a revisit of the earlier accounts of the use of the word nagah is needed.

First, by way of reminder, Abram was told:

> Genesis 15:13,14 *And He said unto Abram, Know of a surety that thy seed shall be a stranger in a land that is not theirs, and shall serve them: and they shall afflict them four hundred years; and also that nation, whom they shall serve, will I judge: and afterward shall they come out with great substance.*

YHVH is basically saying that He would separate the Sons of Abraham from the sons of Pharaoh-Egypt after a multi-generational scattering! In addition, those who have been scattered, seemingly outcasts, would generations later become a Nation whose ancestral patrimony would be called into question by those Elitists who falsely lay claim to their blood rights. A Nation who, in these Last Days would be gathered from the 4-

corners of the World in anticipation of a Greater mass Exodus with one goal in mind – accessing the Promised Inheritance!

Their return to Torah coupled with an indefatigable will to keep the Sabbath and other Holy Convocations would become certifiable evidence attested to by the Manifestation of Supernatural demonstrations of majesty and power identifying them as the aboriginal pure stock – The Sons of Elohiym - and as the Promised Heirs - thus able to access their Inheritance as Firstborn! This sounds much like the Promise to gather the outcasts of Israel and bring them into the Promised – Debar [The place where words become seed] Land.

Once More, Why Kill the Firstborn?

Scholars have wrestled with such for millennia. For instance, Israel was later told to go into the Promised Land a.k.a. 'The Land of Canaan' and kill all the men, women, children as well as, the cattle of the 7-Nations, an event that provokes people to call YHVH a harsh and brutal Deity. Yet, it is evident to those who are willing to look into the Ancient Text that He was acting to drastically cut off the seedline of the Nephylim in order to prevent Israel from comingling their seed with those hybridized Chimera!

I think our evidence bears the question: Is it possible that this 10th plague specifically targeted the hybridized seed – those offspring of the Pharonic, Egyptian and their union with the Fallen Ones? Could this be why Moshe is called to certify, witness against them? If anyone would have had that knowledge Moshe, who had been privy to the throne of Egypt would. To this end, on a smaller scale, some of the Sages teach that the Egyptians had indeed engaged in natural, physical, adulterous affairs and as a result there were often several 'firstborn' in each house. Children from different fathers!

If what we've alleged is true, then there should have been 'firstborn' within the houses of Israel who merited this plague as well, had not the blood been applied to their doorposts! The list includes such notables as Miriam, the Eldest sister of Moshe and Aaron. Again, the names suggest as much. Pray look...

**Kindly note: Miriam, in Hebrew H#4813, מרים, Miryam, is a woman whose name even the translators render as 'Rebellion'. If we break it apart we have Mar-rebellion or Mar - bitter and Yam – waters. From which we get 'Bitter Waters' as in the Waters of Jealousy! This reminds us of the test of marital fidelity in Numbers 5, where the wife who is accused of adultery is given the bitter waters of judgment to drink.

This 'Cup of Jealousy' was a concoction consisting of a 'handwriting of ordinances' – i.e. the accusation against her consisting of the specific law being broken – and written upon a skin parchment – the ink is washed with water (Much like the ritual known as the Ashes of the Red Heifer) that is comingled with the dust of the Tabernacle floor. The Cup is then poured over the parchment, washing or blotting out the accusations into a cup of 'bitterness', which she was made to drink. If guilty her belly and thigh rots out, if not, she conceives seed!

Another hidden clue is found in the primordial rite of 'Threshold Covenanting' an act demonstrated in the Pesach ritual of applying blood to the doorposts and lintels of each Israelite house. The ritual had its roots in the ancient Marriage Covenant. At this time, in keeping with that same Threshold Covenant - YHVH took to Himself the Virgin of Israel as His Bride, in effect doing more than bypassing each house that had blood applied and actually entering into the house to her! Much as Ezekiel speaks:

> Ezekiel 16:8 *Now when I passed by you, and looked upon you, behold, thy time was the time of love; and I spread my skirt over you, and covered thy nakedness:*

> *Yes, I sware unto you, and entered into a covenant with you, saith YHVH, and you become mine!*

In Israel's case, though, there is controversy here regarding the specific Hebrew letter formed by the blood of the Passover Lamb applied to the lintels of the house, some saying Chet, some Tav. However, it is my opinion that it could have been in the form of the letter 'Hey' – ה – in effect, applying the same breath, breathing, spirit, and declaration of renewal as that of the letter ה added to Abram and Sarai! This changing of names demonstrated an exchanging of positions, a new status for the participants! Thus, the Paschal blood, like the Ashes of the Red Heifer protected the Guilty Bride from death as both the Lamb and the Red Heifer die in their stead!

Following the above pattern, as our Messiah Yahshua is scourged before His execution, it is my opinion that His SKIN – PARCHMENT representing the written Law-Torah - was comingled with His own blood and later, water, with the dust of the original ADAMAH, and poured out upon the Altar of the Earth-Adamah to eradicate the guilt of the Niddah Bride and to restore the truth instead of the Accusation of Adulterous Bride and bastard sons by testifying to the world with the inscription upon the stake: **Yahshua H'notzri V'Meleck H'Yehudiym!** In effect giving us the 4-letter Tetragrammaton YHVH! I believe He makes specific reference to this Bitter Cup while in agonized prayer in the Garden where He remarks: "If possible let this CUP pass from me, nevertheless, not My will, but Thine be done".

As we continue to look back at the Firstborn Miriam, מרים, we see that her name is only one letter removed from Egypt – מצרים, Miriam missing the letter 'Tzade.' It is said that Tzade represents righteousness and judgment. The Sages say it has two heads: Indicating choice. It also connotes the Tzadeq One – The Righteous One – The Messiah Yahshua who, like Israel went down into the Womb of Miryam – the belly or womb of bitter waters – to rectify the choice made in the garden by Adam and

Eve-Chavah. His choice restores us to a new Status, that of serving YHVH. The letter Tzade is connected to the Zodiacal sign of Aquarius, the Water Bearer! The One Who Drinks The Cup of Jealousy for us!

It is my contention that this 10th plague – death of the 1st-born – was a direct response to the attempt of Pharaoh and Egypt to compromise the seed of Israel and became the tool used to bring about their restoration as both Bride and Firstborn Son! As we fast-forward to the coming Greater Exodus, I assert that the spirit of Pharaoh and Egypt, both evincing an Anti-Messiah typology, rests upon the Elite of the world and in particular, the Powers-That-Be who currently govern the enslaved of the UNITED STATES OF AMERICA!

If in doubt of the above statement, one need only read and study the 14th amendment carefully. If done, you would find that all 'Citizens' of the corporate entity called The UNITED STATES OF AMERICA are in fact, deemed "enemy combatants" and enslaved by the very document that many flout as the 'Constitution'. In conclusion of this chapter…

That Being Said, Here Are Some Established Facts

Fact #1: *You are in Egypt/Babylon, not Kansas Dorothy!* Your rightful inheritance was stolen from you through the Birth certificates, S.S. numbers, Marriage licenses etc. and monetized globally in order to use your SWEAT EQUITY as slaves to fund the International cabal that will shortly put into power the Last Pharaoh! The Anti-Messiah!

Fact #2: As we speak, the Planetary Medical Crime Syndicate already has the capability to manipulate your DNA in monstrous ways that would chill the blood of the staunchest man. They use various mediums such as EMF, Vaccines, Genetically Modified –

artificial food; medical devices deigned as 'tests', and transplanted human/chimerical organs. They exploit the basic desire for an understanding of our ethnic origins and offer DNA testing as a means to access that. Few realize the results of those tests are stored for their use.

Fact #3: The Powers –That - Be use their might to legislate morality, and thus, disenfranchise the Conservative Believing Community. Their ideals exploit the naïve, bully the ignorant and stamp out any and all resistance to their agenda, which is to depopulate and destroy all those 'animals' that feed off them. The terms 'human', male and female, though not commonly known to most, are simply ancient linguistic double-speak methods designating the baser Citizen as an animal!

Fact #4: They utilize every method to divide and thus, conquer the populace (A House divided against itself cannot stand) the MOST DANGEROUS OF WHICH is the religious zeal of those who have little knowledge of the above, and thus fuel the fires of their own demise!

Just this past week, I was accused by a couple that are a well-known praise and worship team - Messianic Leaders - of being an occultist, demonically influenced and guilty of manipulating others to do something these two deemed impossible: Simply - "Come out of Babylon". They felt it is merely a spiritual endeavor and that we must play along with those who enslave us. Yet, it is a fact: Israel physically came out of Egypt and there is a REMNANT who will shortly, physically, spiritual and financially, extricate themselves from spiritual Egypt and Babylon in the Greater Exodus!

In closing Chapter 11: You are entitled to an inheritance bought and paid for by Messiah Yahshua - Your own "Promised Land". Yet, if your mind is still enslaved, i.e. you have little to no knowledge of how to extricate yourself from Egypt – Babylon, it will not matter if the physical restraints are removed, you will remain in bondage! YHVH has already released the Exodus Plagues upon the earth in increments that will continue to grow in intensity! The effort to awaken the House of Israel is in process. These 10 plagues will overlap and each bolster the other culminating in the destruction of those ILLIGITIMATE BASTARD SONS WHO CALL THEMSELVES THE FIRSTBORN while the True Sons of Elohiym will exit Egypt/Babylon and begin their journey toward restoration!

Chapter 12

The Red Sea Crossing
The Exodus Plagues Continued

Exodus 14:1 - 15:22

Though we finished looking at all 10 of the quote "plagues" it is my opinion that there remains yet one plague for us to consider in the final judgment of Egypt as the Greater Exodus begins. I refer to it as the incident at the Red Sea. We will look closer here and hopefully, link together what many consider an altogether apocryphal and figurative story with what I believe is a parallel shown us in the works of John the Revelator!

Is it Possible That a Future Red Sea Crossing, of a sort that will stagger most, is in our immediate future? If so, will it happen literally, in other words, will we all gather at the same location and cross over, or will there be a figurative crossing by multitudes from out of the Nations who will cross an even greater 'SEA'. These questions beg an answer! What's yours?

Before moving on, surely we must agree: These Exodus plagues are rehearsed again on an amplified scale during what many call the 'Great Tribulation'. Thus, their blueprints should follow the same context, patterns, chronology, purposes, as well as, who the judgments are directed against, and finally, who dispatches them.

Take care Reader, that you make no mistake, the judgment has begun!

**Please take note: The timing of this event is 3-days after the Pesach lamb is slain (Nissan 14th) making the crossing occur on Nissan 17th, the same time as the resurrection of Yahshua and the resting of Noah's ark on Mt. Ararat, which is translated as: 'The Curse Reversed'. It would seem then, that a unique association exists with this 'Crossing' as well, reversing the curse of slavery and opening the Matrix to those Free-Born Sons of the Most High!

Israel Camps Before Crossing

Exodus 14:2 tells us Israel is commanded by YHVH to stop and camp at Pihahiroth, between Migdol and the sea, over against Baalzephon: These names have been consistently mistranslated in my opinion. So, let's examine them.

- Pihahiroth, H#6367 פיהחרת

    Rendered by some as the "place where the sedge grows". In my opinion, it is a poor translation at best. As a phrase, Pi comes from the root Peh, meaning mouth, to speak, command, the edge, border or a boundary. Next, the letter 'Hey' is a preposition giving us 'the'. This leaves us with חרת, chorowt, and the plural of chowr, which derives from the Chet-Resh-Resh, charar root, and means to be or become free, freedom. This gives us: The Boundary, a border to freedom! Implying that Israel has yet to cross the Red Sea in order to experience their true deliverance.

- Migdol, H#4024 מגדול

    It is translated as 'tower', the Mem indicates a womb as in source of origin, leaving us with gadal, meaning great or strong. It carries the idea of a 'collective strength'. You'll remember this word from Genesis 11 and the tower – or Migdol of Babel, where all gathered who were collectively 'in one mind and one accord'. Further, you'll recall the woman out of whom Yahshua cast 7-devils, Mary Magdalene, her last name carries this Migdol root and indicates Miryam of the Tower.

**Remember this!

- Baalzephon, H#1189   בעל צפון

    It is defined as: Lord of the North. But, once again, we have a compound word. To be candid, Baal has gotten a bad rap being associated with a Pagan deity and as here is most often translated as 'lord or husband'; yet, as seen in Jeremiah 3:14 Baal can also mean to have dominion, to marry, as in YHVH marrying Israel. While the second part of the name, 'zephon' though translated as 'north' can also mean that which is hidden, concealed, to treasure, stored up, a secret.

From an Egyptian perspective Israel is now trapped between the wilderness and the Sea. Yet, the prophetic names of the above places tell us that YHVH had another plan. Their extrapolated definition indicates: *"I will bring you, My concealed treasure, My hidden Bride, to the place where I will reveal My Strength – The Strong Tower – and bring you across the boundary to freedom!"*

In stark contrast, as the Adversary is wont to do, here is what Pharaoh says in opposition - Exodus 14:3: *They are entangled in the land and the wilderness has shut them in.* Once again, the KJV gives little input, but look at the language of Creation.

- Entangled, H#943　　בוך　　Buch

   It is defined as disturbed, confused, perplexed.

- Wilderness, H#4057,　　מדבר　　Midbar

   It is simply rendered as 'wilderness' here. However, the Mem prefix indicates a womb, and debar is a Promised Word. What word had Israel been recently promised if not, FIRSTBORN STATUS?

- Shut in, H#5462　　סגר　　Sagar

   Though it is translated as 'shut or closed up' it can also mean to deliver up!

The word 'buch' above has the same two-letter root stem - Bet-Kaf - as Bechor a Hebrew word indicating Firstborn! It seems Pharaoh thought Israel was wandering around in confusion with no hope in which to demonstrate their newly found 'Firstborn' status and recent deliverance as slaves. However, YHVH has brought them here and revealing that a *'birthing of His Promise to make them His First Born is about to occur'*! In keeping with the Prophetic Picture, the path through the Red Sea literally becomes the birth canal and figuratively, Israel is resurrected – born again – on the other side! Still, there remain other less obvious, and altogether as powerful connections that are prophesying of our own future crossing over and us!

One ambiguous link looks remarkably like the prophetic declaration of Genesis 3:15 where a battle between 2-distinct seed lines is first prophesied. It seems it is found occurring here at the Red Sea crossing as well. If you recall Genesis 3:15, this declaration is made by YHVH to Adam and Eve-Chavah after their encounter with the Nachash – That Old Serpent - The Enchanter – One who enslaves by his words! **There has never**

been a generation more defrauded by enchanting words than ours!

Most think this verse is speaking of future generations to come, like Jacob and Esau and indeed it is; yet, it is also grammatically speaking to the 2 separate seed now within the womb of Chavah - Cain and Abel! It seems here at the Red Sea crossing, that Pharaoh and his army, like those two opposing sons, also enter the same womb as Israel! In response, YHVH deals strongly with the counterfeit! Rest assured dear Reader! We will see a future demonstration of these same phenomena a scientific anomaly known as – *Hetero Paternal Super fecundation*: A medical term describing two separate seed in a womb at the same time from two separate fathers!

The Significance of the Red Sea

Much of what is known of the ancient name applied to this body of water is obscured, albeit, I believe intentionally, in order to obfuscate what is surely a place of central importance not only in our Biblical texts, but in the 'doomsday' scenarios conjured by many students of End-Time prophecy. The KJV texts render it: Red Sea, H#5488, סוף H#3220, ים Yam Suph. Though various translators portray this as; a Sea of Reeds, a small, boggy, miry body of water – it is frankly, a definition that doesn't fit Israel's actual place of crossing. This 'Sea of Reeds' is genuinely, quite far removed from the actual site. Again, Roman Catholicism has colored much of this debate.

However, you and I have never settled for conventional ideology! The translation of Yam Suph does not merit the word 'RED'. It has nothing to do with that specific color. But, ancient texts nevertheless connect the red color with this Sea, why? Since, we've portrayed a future 'twins in the womb scenario', at a future Red Sea crossing, is it possible that a return of Esau-Edom - which means Red - to the Womb here at the Sea

Crossing in order to masquerade as Jacob could possibly be hidden within? If you recall, throughout their wilderness journeys a *'mixed multitude'* always seemed to be found at the center of every controversy!

Side Bar

Perhaps we should look at this term: The Hebrew is ערב רב, ereb rab – Mixed multitude. The root takes on the idea of taking a pledge or to pledge in exchange. If we look at other passages where the expression is used (Jeremiah 25:20, 50:37, Ezekiel 30:5) the term is consistently translated within the context of war and those who're killed in battle. Thus, it seems that these 'mixed multitude' were armed mercenaries and who at some time, perhaps conveniently during the decimation of Egypt's military power had intermingled with Israel leaving with them at the Exodus!

In support of our position of 2-warring seedline in the womb here, the text in Exodus 12:38 says *'and a mixed multitude went up'* - וגם-ערב רב עלה V'gam-ereb rab alah...this phrase has a gematria of 628, the same as the Hebrew word bechorath, indicating "first-born"!

Who Were/Are This Mixed Multitude?

There are scholars such as *W. Zimmerli, Ezekiel 2: A Commentary on the Book of the Prophet Ezekiel* along with others, who also agree that these were mixed individuals who had assimilated into Israel by CONVERTING! Will a future Red Sea event also involve the purging of a mixed multitude from the House of Israel?

**You'd do well to remember this!

Where then, and for what purpose in this study, did the idea of a 'red' Sea as a name come? How does it figure in our paradigm of the End-Times? In answer, there are age-old records of the Edomite-Idumean colonization of places like the ancient city of Tyre by a King referred to as "Erythras" [Eh-ryth-ras] meaning 'Red' who was said to have come from the area now called the 'Red Sea'. In corroboration, Rashi in his comments on Genesis 25:23 states that Esau – Edom meaning RED, colonized Tyre! Further, an affinity between the two (Tyre and Edom) is shown in Amos 1:9,10.

Another Ancient Source: Flavius Philostratus was a Greco-Roman scholar that dwelt in the ancient Phoenician city of Tyre shown above. In his seminal work The Life of Apollonius, he explains that the "Sea called Erythra" was taken from the name of the King of Erythras. (170-245 AD).[24]

Moreover, the word סוף, Suph, as in Yom Suph, has no etymological connection to either Red or Reed. In fact, some linguists believe it implies 'the edge, border, extremity or end'. This would be consistent with ancient folklore describing the Red Sea as "The Sea At The End of The World". Literally, a spiritual dimensional gateway into the Eternal located at the world's edge; or perhaps, the Sea that must be confronted at the End of the Age?

This is highly plausible as it borders the ancient tectonic plate rifts of both Africa and Arabia and could have been called such because of those who witnessed the landmasses separating in the days of Peleg (Genesis 10:25) in his days the earth was divided. If accurate and in this context, this rift will once again become prominent during the "Tribulation Period" as the tectonic rupture extends into Jerusalem underneath the Kidron Valley to the Mt. of Olives the place that is said to split at the 2nd coming of Messiah!

---

[24] https://religion.wikia.org/wiki/Erythraean_Sea
No direct quote. Attribution only.

It is also worth noting that the area where the Fissure has formed is called the 'Afar' Rift or 'Afar Triangle' and said to have been the place of the origin of man's creation. The ethnic groups called 'Afar' who live in that area say that 'Afar' means best or first!

Could the etymological root of this word Afar be related to the word that which comes from – H#6083, עפר, the dust of the Adamah that Adam is created out of? Further, could the formation of a new Land Mass in this Afar Rift Area during the Tribulation possibly expose the what was once the Ancient Gan-Garden of Eden, in effect fulfilling on a physical level the prophecy of Genesis 3:19 ...*for dust-**afar** thou art and unto dust-**afar** that shalt return...* Perhaps hinting at a People called afar – dust who will return to the Afar of the Adamah that was this pre-exilic Eden?

Finally, as we scrutinize the origin of this Red Sea's name, we must remember the encounter of Jacob and Esau as seen from Genesis 25:30 where in his famished condition Esau asks Jacob to: *"Feed me, I pray thee, with that same red pottage: for I am faint: therefore his name was called **Edom-RED**"* [Bold capitals supplied by author] The word used for 'feed' is interesting too, as it appears only 1-time in the Tanak: H#3938, לעט, la`at, indicating to swallow something greedily, to devour.

La`at is preceded by several cognate words with the Lamed-Ayin root indicating to mock, deride, and to scorn; it strongly hints at attacking a person's words and position. Is it possible that Esau scorns Jacob, mocking his junior familial position as one without inheritance, because he believes he has a greater vessel offering him more power and authority than the trifling [sarcasm mine] Firstborn birthright of the House of Abraham & Isaac? (The Sages add a bit of clarity in their comments here, as you'll learn later)

Will a future ESAU confront the House of Jacob/Israel by deriding their efforts in the gathering of the Outcasts for an exodus out of Egypt/Babylon/Rome, denying their title or birthrights all the while asserting their own presumed right of Firstborn Inheritance?

Further, as we continue looking, the KJV translators add the word 'pottage', which is not in the original text, in fact, the English word translated 'red' – adom itself is repeated twice in Hebrew: הלאיטני מן-האדם האדם h'leyitni min-h'adom h'adom. The doubling of the above word 'adom' is noteworthy. Especially when we consider the root stem of la`at – Lamed-Tet, which hints at secrecy, enchantment and was the word used to describe the Magicians of Pharaoh! Have you noticed how this word 'enchantment' just casually keeps popping up?

Lastly, we'll consider the hyphened word 'min' - מִן, which can mean 'from, out of, on account of, to separate or expel, yet it can also indicate to apportion, part out. This extrapolation adds a bit of a twist to "feed me, I pray thee, with that same red pottage" – It just as easily could also have read: *I will swallow down; devour, by secret enchantments that which was apportioned the Adam – The Adam!* There's that word 'enchantment' again...

While the above is not conventional thinking, it is consistent with what some Rabbis say regarding why Esau was famished – that he was running for his life after having killed Nimrod and having taken the 'skin-garment' cloak once said to have belonged to Adam, a garment that Nimrod had long held! Could this supposedly powerful garment have been the Secret Vessel Esau places his expectations of World dominance in, rather than his own Right of Firstborn in His Father's house?

**See Jasher 27:1-13. Though you may not think so, there is a group today who place just as much store in such icons. For instance, the ancient cup or chalice that Jesus drank from and the spearhead used to pierce His side. Let's back up a bit and explain…

In Genesis 1:26-28 we find an eternal promise made to Adam and divided into 2-distinct parts: A Dominion mandate and a Fruitfulness mandate. (Be fruitful and have dominion) Because of the work of Yahshua in restoring both, the combined Promises of Firstborn Inheritance is achievable by all those who worship Him. On the other hand, those carnal individuals seeking the same through their own methods of rebellion rather than following YHVH's plan have embraced a secret, forbidden knowledge found at the Tree of Carnal Knowledge – also known as - The Tree of divine ENCHANTMENTS! Oops, there is that word enchantment again!

Through Esau there is another unique latter-day connection brought to us by his grandson Eliphaz and great-grandson Amalek! (Discussed earlier in this book) Therefore, it should come as no surprise that a great conflict between Esau and Jacob ensues at the close of the age. Will it be at a future Red Sea encounter? Could it be physically, and figuratively as well?

Take note of what the prophet Obadiah has to say in regard to this. You should carefully consider, though only 1-chapter long, its entirety is devoted to the destruction of Esau. Interestingly, Obadiah was from the house of Esau! Verse 18 *Then the house of Jacob will be a fire and the house of Joseph a flame; but the house of Esau will be as stubble. And they will set them on fire and consume them, so that there will be no survivor of the house of Esau, for YHVH has spoken!* Why does this future prophecy mention JOSEPH?

Putting this into proper context is imperative and hopefully, will explain much!

This End-Times conflict will include JOSEPH who I believe (In the stead of both Judah and Levi) is entitled to the Birthright and

PRIESTHOOD – In this role He prefigures Messiah and as such found unlocking the connection to Melchizedek going all the way back to Genesis 14 where a transfer occurs between Shem/Melchizedek, the Priest of El Elyon and Abraham and where we find what I believe is a deliberate mistranslation.

> Genesis 14:19,20: *And he blessed him, and said, "Blessed be Abram of the most high God, possessor of heaven and earth. And blessed be the most high God, which hath delivered thine enemies into thy hand. And he gave him tithes of all.*

**Note: Once again, it is this Melchizedek speaking to the subject Abram; In other words, he blessed him, and he gave to him. As Melchizedek continues his blessing it becomes evident that it is HE WHO GAVE TITHES TO ABRAM!

Thus, Jacob through Joseph continues the Birthright, which includes the Melchizedec Priestly role and this restored office will be made prominent as Joseph confronts Esau who will be found in the near future hiding in the garments of Jacob and I believe, concealed among the ROMAN - Levitical Cabal. He, who will once again seek to establish his dominion mandate through the supposed 'Skin Coat' of Adam, which is an effort to validate the legitimacy of animal sacrifice and thus, Levitical inheritance, though it was never intended that the blood of animals could atone for man's sin! This issue of animal sacrifice is central to the building of the coming 3rd-Temple and it is essential that you understand it to be the most divisive enterprise facing those of us who contend that the Temple that should be our focus, must be ONE NOT MADE WITH HANDS AND THAT NO ANIMAL NEED BE SLAUGHTERED TO SUFFICE THE NEED FOR REDEMPTION PAID FOR BY YAHSHUA!

Look what Malachi has to say regarding Esau's plans to 'return and build':

Malachi 1:4 *Though Edom says, we have been beaten down, but we will return and build up the ruins: thus says the Lord of Hosts, They may build, but I will tear down/ and men will call them the wicked territory, and the people toward whom YHVH is indignant forever.*

The Final Temple that will be built is one, not made with hands! The 3rd-Temple is not it and I believe the wrath of the Most High will be kindled against it! As we move forward in our investigation of the Red Sea Plague, and since we don't believe in coincidence, we must consider therefore, the gematria of la`at (feed me) shown as 109, and seen with the same value as מגניו, magennayav, the root of which is Magen – shield. By the way, the most famous of all families belonging to the Illuminist, Secret - Elite World Powers is that of Rothschild – Red Shield. Is there an Esau-Nimrod connection? Wait for it…

As we pursue this thread linking the Red Sea to Edom-Esau, it is also worth noting that ancient tradition says that one of the early leaders of Edom was referred to as: "Duke Magdiel" from Genesis 36:43. It was this Duke according to that same tradition that is said to have founded ancient Rome. Let's examine the name.

- Duke, H#441 אלוּף *'Alluph*

    It indicates a familiar friend, a tamed animal, a chieftain. It comes from H#502 אלף, 'alowph, meaning to teach by association.

- Magdiel, H#4025 מגדיאל

    It is a compound of El and meged, translated here as noble, eminent. Some relate it to maggid, a teacher. Ironically, the Targum of Jonathan says this Duke was called Magdiel from the name of a city, which had a strong Migdol or tower!

**Remember ancient lore that Esau killed Nimrod, the builder of the Tower of Babble?

We must ask ourselves 'what was the man teaching, that led to the distinction of his being accredited with the founding of Rome'?

It is also interesting to note the etymological relationship of Magdiel with two prominent words also connected to End-Times prophecy, one of which we've already mentioned – Migdol – tower and Megiddo/Megiddon as in Har-Megiddon or Armageddon as the English translation gives us!

Additionally, it is also significant that the Greek name for the Red Sea is: Mare Erythraeum. (Sea Red) From the former 'mare' - we get 'Maritime' as in the *"Law of the Sea"* also known as Admiralty Law. Like Israel in Egypt, today all the world's Citizens are under the international control of the Roman/Edomite/Crown of England junta who have enslaved them and stolen their birthrights by having implemented this 'Law of the Sea'. It is this crossing of this most powerful SEA that must be the final stage before the Greater Exodus truly begins, along with, the securing of our freedom. By the way, the word 'crossing' can also indicate crossbreeding and hybridization! What's significant about this latter phrase, 'crossbreeding and hybridization'?

Remember Mary Magdalene from Point I Above?

Perhaps you'll recall that we pointed out the relationship between the tower – Migdol and the name associated with this Mary from Magdalah. It is interesting to say the least, and there are many who adhere to the legend believing wholeheartedly in its lies. For instance, The Illuminists would have you believe that Yahshua didn't die on the execution stake, rather, He was taken down and later, married this Mary of the Migdol, (Try saying that fast 3-times!) creating an alternative bloodline known as the Merovingian Bloodline that would open the doors for a Dominance Mandate executed by the Crown of England, the Papacy and their rogue Jewish cohorts!

In the near future, there will emerge both political and religious Leaders out of this Tribunal who will claim a divine connection to Messiah, but, who will have actually sprung up out of what many call an "extra-terrestrial race", which is merely a Fallen Angelic or demonic hybridization of the Two! This lineage will produce the ANTI-MESSIAH and will once again attempt to generate the 1st of two seedline, both within one womb – Esau and Jacob/Joseph!

Ironically, together the Roman Church and the Crown of England are known for their affinity toward The Cloak of Adam - Cloak of Nimrod – The Cloak of EDOM - THE RED CLOAK – The Rothschild – Red Shield! Can you remember the Red Coats of your history lessons? It is this same secretive plan woven into much of what is held as inherently 'Jewish' today. For instance, the beloved song 'If I Were a Rich Man' from the popular musical Fiddler on the Roof was actually a spin off of *'Ven ikh bin Roytshild'* or 'If I were a Rothschild' a 19th century story by Sholem Aleichem, a man struggling to keep his family within the Jewish faith...

The deception is almost complete and rather than expose the truth and risk being called 'Anti-Semitic', many in the Hebrew Roots, Messianic Faith are, more often than not, seduced as a result! Looking forward, we must remember John the Revelator's declaration to the churches of Smyrna and Philadelphia at the behest of the Ruach:

> Revelation 2:9 *...I know the blasphemy of them which say they are Jews, and are not, but are the synagogue of Satan. 3:9 Behold, I will make them of the synagogue of Satan, which say they are Jews, and are not, but do lie...*

These verses have polarized many in today's Churches and additionally, the Hebrew Roots and Messianic groups as well! With the renewed fervor associated with the return to their 'Jewishness' many have succumbed to the controlling Powers who want no public attention given to the Protocols of the Learned Elders of Zion! At the risk of being accused of an anti-Jewish author, let me state that I firmly attest that I Love the House of Israel, I wholeheartedly embrace and keep the Torah, the Sabbath, the Holy Convocations and long for the reunion of both the House of Judah and the House of Ephraim. That being said, there is a counterfeit in the house that must be exposed! Please take note of the following dissection of Revelation 2:9 and 3:9. It will open your eyes...prayerfully.

- Smyrna, Gk#4668

    It is actually a name derived from the ancient spice called myrrh, a bitter and fragrant spice that was originally used to mark the Tabernacle, but which came to be used to proclaim olfactorily, the consummation of a marriage.

- Philadelphia, Gk#5359

    It is translated as; City of brotherly love. Really? With a bit more digging our efforts give us philos, from the Greek indicating loving, sophos, to be wise, in short, loving wisdom. Further, we have adelphus, from the ancient Greek 'adelphos' meaning born of the same womb! If we combine the two we get: *Wisdom of the brothers born of the same womb!* Surely, by now you don't believe in coincidence?

Could this ancient hoax – the end goal of which was the marrying together of the Plans of the Nachash-Enchanter to bring forth sons who would be 'like the gods' with an unsuspecting, primed for seduction group! If we rightly divide the Word, an abundance of ample proof exists that these plans had already have been at work among the early Believing Community and the Prophet of Revelation puts his finger directly on it, exposing its origins! But for whom was this epistle of Revelation written? YOU and I!

To get even more specific, the construction of the 3rd-Temple will ratify this unholy marriage covenant, which will, I believe, lead to the same event referred to as the Covenant of Peace declared between the Anti-Messiah and Israel.

> Daniel 9:27 *And he shall confirm the covenant with many for one week: and in the midst of the week he shall cause the sacrifice and the oblation to cease, and for the overspreading of abominations he shall make it desolate, even until the consummation, and that determined shall be poured upon the desolate.*
>
> 1Thessalonians 5:3 *For when they say Peace and safety; then sudden destruction cometh upon them, as travail upon a woman with child; and they shall not escape)*

The birthing pains are similar to Israel being in the amniotic waters of the RED SEA and facing imminent destruction by the Last Pharaoh!

Ask Yourself This

Most End-Times scholars acknowledge a "Greater Exodus" comprised of those Outcasts of Israel scattered into the 4-corners of the world. However, if we believe that Satan attempts to counterfeit every notable plan of YHVH then we should expect a "Greater Exodus" from the House of Esau as well! I contend that is exactly what is happening with those fulfilling the prophecy of:

> Genesis 9:27 *YHVH shall enlarge Japheth, and he shall dwell in the tents of Shem; and Canaan shall be his servant.*

It is my opinion that the Gog-Magog war - so often attributed to an invasion by the armies of the Nation of Russia could in fact be an assault – a.k.a. ALIYAH - of those Edomite-Khazarim-Ashkenazi imposters born out of Japheth's son called Magog!

For generations Religious Scholars have taught a great conflagration consisting of the National armies of Russia and others would be assaulting the isolated Jewish State of Israel in the supposed great Gog-Magog war! I believe that we've misinterpreted those texts and the assault actually began in earnest in 1948. This has been part of the cleverly concealed Zionist plans to purge the Ashkenazi Khazar from those Nations in a veiled attempt to overwhelm the Land with Esau instead of Jacob! This is commonly referred to as making 'Aliyah'.

These individuals are coming out of Magog, the prince of Rosh – Russia, Meshech – Moscow, Tubal-Tubolsk, and Togarmah – Eastern Europe, the U.S.A. etc. By the way, Aliyah was a ancient term used to describe Joseph taking Jacob's bones back to the Land, not those of an imposter!

Yes, the Red Sea crossing of Exodus 14 did really happen! Yes, it was a literal crossing of a body of water, but there were, in addition, powerful, covert and prophetic details that would become a mirror for us to look into in order that we not succumb to the divine enchantments of these END DAYS! In summation, please see:

> Matthew 24:23,24 *Then if any man shall say unto you, Lo, here is Messiah, or there; believe it not. For there*

shall arise false Messiahs, and false prophets, and shall shew great signs and wonders; insomuch that, if it were possible, they shall deceive the very elect.

The Greek Septuagint uses the same word above for deceive, Gk.#4105, plan-ah`-o, to cause to stray, lead astray, as in our opening text here in Exodus 14:3 *For Pharaoh will say of the children of Israel, They are **entangled**-plan-ah`-o in the land and the wilderness has shut them in.* The Hebrew word used says more!

- Entangled, H#943   בוך   Buch

It means disturbed, confused, perplexed.

The word 'buch' above has the same two-letter root stem - Bet-Kaf - as Bechor indicating Firstborn! Pharaoh thought Israel was wandering around in confusion with no hope in which to demonstrate their newly found 'Firstborn' status and deliverance as slaves. However, YHVH has brought them here and revealing that a *'birthing of His Promise to make them His First Born is about to occur'*! The path through the Red Sea literally becomes the birth canal and figuratively, Israel catches the heel of Esau and is resurrected – born again – on the other side!

In closing, this journey we've begun together has by no means been fruitless. I've gained a renewed respect and awe for the Creator's purpose in sharing these truths with you dear Reader. I know that much of what has been written within has never been seen this way before, at least not in our lifetime. We must awaken to the deception and take a stand while we still have the luxury of time. You're reading this book, not by accident I might add, and I would be remiss if I didn't share with you that YHVH has plans for you. Yes, you! Plans for good and not for evil, to bring you to an expected destination! (Jeremiah 29:11)

Take care to meditate on what I've shared with you. Measure it against the Scriptures from Genesis to Revelation. Pray earnestly and with humility and listen to the Voice of the Ruach – His Spirit! If this is Truth – and I believe it is – then it can stand scrutiny! There are going to be dark days ahead indeed and they've already started! Many will be swept away in the current of apathy. I challenge you to rise above the ordinary and take the place that has been created and waiting for you! Your destiny awaits. Take this material and share it. Don't be afraid to Stand!

Lastly, our commitment to you has already been printed in this work. There are countless hours of prayer, study and sweat steeped into these pages. We extend it further by supplying our contact information in order to answer questions that you may not find answers to here. We are here for you! We're waiting for you to come home and the Reunion of the House of Israel will be our finest hour!

Hugs and Squeezes from,
The MannaCrew!

www.ingramcontent.com/pod-product-compliance
Lightning Source LLC
Chambersburg PA
CBHW070546170426
43201CB00012B/1742